What others are saying about this book:

After reading *Kate's Journey*, I added Kate Adamson to my list of heroes. Her life of courage and tenacity, despite the odds, is an inspirational lesson for us all.
— SUSAN JEFFERS, PH.D., AUTHOR OF *FEEL THE FEAR AND DO IT ANYWAY* AND *EMBRACING UNCERTAINTY*

Kate's story is both inspiring and informative. I highly recommend it for health professionals and especially for students who are seeking to understand what the patient with a severe neurological injury actually goes through. This book effectively counters the conventional wisdom that after a severe stroke a person's life is over. Kate demonstrates that determination and strength of will are the most important elements of a rehabilitation program.
— JAMES GORDON, EdD, PT, ASSOCIATE PROFESSOR AND CHAIR UNIVERSITY OF SOUTHERN CALIFORNIA, DEPARTMENT OF BIOKINESIOLOGY AND PHYSICAL THERAPY

I hope people will read your book because it will help them very much.
— ART BUCHWALD

Kate wouldn't have survived if she hadn't been in excellent shape before her stroke. Her physical condition and will to live pulled her through.
— DR. STEVEN KOLODNEY

Reading *Kate's Journey* allowed me to reflect and really understand the impact that we as healthcare professionals have on people who have incurred catastrophic events. This book allowed me to appreciate the power of the human spirit; it is a lesson I will draw upon my entire life.
— COVEY J. LAZOURAS, DPT

Kate takes us on a journey from loss and despair to rebirth and hope with humor, grace and faith. A remarkable triumph.
— BONNIE FRANKLIN / ACTRESS

If you ever wondered if 'miracles' are real, all you need to do is listen to the amazing and very real story of what Kate has come through. Kate's story will renew your faith and fill you with the same joy that helped her overcome life's heartaches.
— JAY JONES / TELEVISION HOST AND PRODUCER, TRINITY BROADCASTING NETWORK

Kate wants to help you. She knows the questions you have and she has the answers because she has been there. Experience counts, you count and this book counts.
—DAN POYNTER, AUTHOR OF THE SELF PUBLISHING MANUAL

Kate's Journey is a profoundly moving story. But even more important, it is a message of hope and inspiration.
— GREGORY J.P. GODEK, AUTHOR OF *1001 WAYS TO BE ROMANTIC*

Kate's Journey won't make you think about how much better off you are than someone else. *Kate's Journey* will help you be so much better than you were. Read it! Live it! Now.
— W MITCHELL, CPAE, AUTHOR OF *IT'S NOT WHAT HAPPENS TO YOU, IT'S WHAT YOU DO ABOUT IT*

What an amazing story! I had no idea what you have been through (and triumphed over) until I started reading *Kate's Journey*. Your description of what you felt and knew during those first days of your stroke are amazing.
— GENE GRIESSMAN, SPEAKER

Kate's Journey is an amazing voyage to the depths of the human spirit. It's a story that helps you celebrate life, and it gives you the strength to overcome any obstacle.
— ED. PETERS, SPEAKER, PRESIDENT, THE 4PROFIT INSTITUTE

As I read your book I marveled at your courage and persistence. You are truly an inspiration for anyone who faces seemingly insurmountable odds. I really think the Lord had a hand in your recovery. The extent of your improvement goes way beyond what a person could accomplish through sheer tenacity. It is truly miraculous.
— M. LAUKAITIS

Your experience with the numerous challenges you faced in your own life has inspired me to overcome my own trials now more than ever. There always comes a time in our life that the daily struggles overwhelm us to no end. I will always remember your strength and courage whenever I feel as if I am carrying the world on my shoulders.
— UELOLENE

Kate's story is a gripping testimony to the intense determination and dedication which enabled her to survive and ultimately triumph over almost unbelievable circumstances. Her book is a very powerful and moving example of the grace of God, and the power of the human spirit. I found myself swept into a maelstrom of emotion as Kate details her experience, from indescribable terror and pain, to the elation and satisfaction of each small step in recovery. I would recommend it to any women facing difficult circumstances. *Kate's Journey* takes the reader for an emotional ride, but leaves you convinced that with hard work, strength of will and the power of God, anything is possible.
— LAURA WARFIELD

This book should be in the home of anyone who has ever had a headache, in the library of every neurologist, and in the hands of every therapist or any health care official that encounters stroke patients. *Kate's Journey* delivers hope through an amazing story of recovery. It was witty and filled with Kate's actual thoughts. I was getting first hand the pain and thoughts that were going through the mind of my own husband. He was at the time living *Kate's Journey*, her nightmare of paralysis and the inability to speak. I recommend reading *Kate's Journey*, a story of recovery and hope, in lieu of books that deliver a message of acceptance of a devastating fate. I prefer the "Never Give Up" message contained within the pages of *Kate's Journey*; a story of bouncing back against all odds. It could happen in the blink of an eye— stroke, paralysis, complete devastation.
— M. JENKINS, SAN DIEGO, CA

This book separates itself from all other books on the market. Kate's story is a tribute to the human spirit in the face of real adversity. Her remarkable journey sweeps you along from the very first page. You won't be able to put this book down, as you are taken back to where she suffered a stroke and was given up for dead. You experience along with Kate what it's like to be a vegetable while awake and aware of everything that is going on—and then the inspiring, triumphant, powerful, and joyful person she is today. I look at life differently, since I read this book. I have an attitude of gratitude, and understanding. I thank you Kate, for writing this book!
— JEAN KRUEGER, AUTHOR OF *WHY THE WEIGHT? DARE TO BE GREAT!*

My sister and I have read your wonderful story of your journey to regain your life! You are a very talented writer. I have been a critical care nurse for 20 years and now a stroke survivor. I had my stroke, October 31, 2001. I lost the ability to use my left arm and leg. Since I knew stroke symptoms well, I pushed for immediate care for my developing stroke. I have taught many trauma lectures and have published on the subjects of traumatic brain injury and spinal cord injury. Your book will make a tremendous difference to other people who are less informed, giving them a much better chance to have a good result. I truly can appreciate your talent as a writer . . . speaker . . . incredible stroke survivor! Thank-you for sharing your story/journey!
— KAREN MICHO STROUPE, RN. ERIE, PA.

Kate's Journey is one of the most compelling and inspirational books I have ever read. One of the employees left this book behind and I happened to glance at it and started reading the first chapter. Well, that was last week, and I just finished reading it today. I felt like I was alongside you cheering you on. Thank you for sharing so much of yourself to the world. I believe we can all learn something that most of us have forgotten about the spirit and will to succeed no matter what the cost. In our system of karate, there is an expression; "Oshi Shinobu", which means to push oneself to the limits of one's ability and yet to continue, to persevere under pressure, and to endure. And to you I say . . . *Oshi Shinoubu!*
— PRINCE LOEFLER, INSTRUCTOR AT THE
   ACADEMY OF JUDO AND KARATE, CA

Kate's personal story of overcoming unbelievable obstacles is an inspiring read! This book is a gift of hope. It will teach anyone how to deal with life's obstacles and how to overcome them with grace and class.

— DEBBIE ALLEN, AWARD-WINNING AUTHOR OF
   CONFESSIONS OF SHAMELESS SELF PROMOTERS

Your book is wonderful. I am deeply moved. My husband had many strokes over the past 9 years and died recently. Your inspiring story reminded me of many similar experiences. You have written an inspiring, encouraging, helpful book, much needed in the world.

— DOTTIE WALTERS, CSP, INTERNATIONAL SPEAKER,
   AUTHOR OF SPEAK AND GROW RICH

KATE'S
Journey

Enjoy the journey

Kate

Dear Mum,

I love you a lot, and I think that I'm so lucky
to have a Mum like you. I'm glad that
you're still here, I like the way you are.

Love,
Rachel (10)

Read this amazing story for inspiration,
tips and examples on how to deal with adversity.
As a kid, you tend to feel carefree and happy.
But what happens when you have to
suddenly become responsible? A life-changing event,
that's what happened in my case. My mum
had a stroke when I was just three years old.
Mum, I'm so glad you survived.

Love,
Stephanie (12)

THE STORY OF A MIRACLE

KATE'S Journey

**Triumph
Over
Adversity**

KATE ADAMSON

NOSMADA PRESS

redondo beach, ca

Published by
NOSMADA PRESS
409 NORTH PACIFIC COAST HIGHWAY
PMB 415
REDONDO BEACH, CA 90277
800-641-KATE

ISBN: 0-9741907-2-1

$19.95 U.S.

WWW.KATESJOURNEY.COM

Publisher's Cataloging-in-Publication Data available upon request.

Printed and bound in the United States of America

Book Design: Dotti Albertine / www.dotdesign.net

This book is dedicated
to stroke survivors and their families
who have suffered and endured strokes.

Stephanie, 12 years / Rachael, 10 years (2004)

CONTENTS

Acknowledgments

THERE ARE MANY PEOPLE who have played a tremendous part in my recovery and today as I continue on this journey called life. Thank you all for enriching my life.

I appreciate my beautiful daughters, Stephanie, and Rachel. Thanks for being you and helping me. I love you dearly. I'm constantly in awe of your strength and courage. I'm so thankful I'm here to see you develop into two well-rounded women.

To Steven, who went an infinite distance to save me. Truly the best possible advocate anyone could have. You make a pretty good doctor for a lawyer! Thanks, for not giving up on me; for that I'll be eternally grateful. I appreciate your help in formulating some of the ideas for the writings in this book and foremost for all your prayers. I know I can count on you, thank you. Thanks for always showing me unconditional love.

Marsha Collins, my baby-sitter for the past eight years. Thank you. You are my 'left' hand. I count on you so much. I appreciate everything you do, right down to making sure there's a tuna sandwich in the fridge for my next day's lunch. You constantly work with me, work around my schedule, and I know I can count on you for every detail.

Dr. Judy Carl, thank you for letting me find out who I am.

Doctor Kolodney, thank you for your patience and compassion. To all the doctors who later came to believe in me and whose skill worked miracles, along with the team of nurses who worked with me. I have a deep appreciation for what nurses do.

To my dear friend Betsy Cogen, my physical therapist in ICU, thank you for treating me like a person when I couldn't communicate. Your kindness and love during those early days is something I shall never forget. What a joy to stay in touch as we do. To Ron Corpus, your physical therapist technician and lastly, thank you Torrance Memorial.

I want to acknowledge Daniel Freeman hospital where I gained back my life. Thank you to everyone who worked with me. I simply cannot mention everyone, but I have not forgotten you and how each person played a part in my recovery. Ron Rooney, you were a great nurse, your humor and care made the unbearable, bearable. A few of you are still in touch with me today, and what a joy to be able to communicate with you. Sister Delores, you kept me grounded, your encouragement was amazing. Doctor Alexander, thank you for believing in me, and leading a great team of therapists to help me reach my goal of walking. Larry Ross, thank you for your help on those community outings. It's wonderful to keep in touch and get to know your wife Kat, who is a gem and the proofreader for this book. Michael Jefferies, my orthopedist, thanks making the best brace that has allowed me to walk again. Your humor kept my spirits up. To all the therapists, thank you for your dedication and believing in me.

Dr Helena Chui, who has become a wonderful friend, and wrote the foreword to the book. Dr. Jefferey Saver, thank you for being a part of the second edition and a friend over the years.

My family in New Zealand, thanks for putting up with me longer than anyone else. We may be a distance apart, but you are all in my heart. Thank you Mum for time you spent with me in those early days of the unknown. Just having you pay attention to the details as only a mother can, meant so much.

The people at Hope Chapel Church who played such a big part in my recovery, they never lost sight of my having a miracle.

A special thanks to Lori Herold, Ron and Rhonda Servine. Thank you to all of you who sat with me, who cooked meals and took care of my daughters. For the many angels who continually prayed for me.

Thanks to Dave Morton, of Tustin, California, for mentoring me in the speaking business and sharing his knowledge and wisdom along the way. To my colleagues with the National Speakers Association throughout the country, thank you. To Dan Poynter, thank you for always taking the time to listen and answer a question. Greg Godek, thanks for sharing ideas with me over coffee and taking my E-mails! To Joel and Bonnie of JD Roberts and associates, you are simply the best media coaches. I want to acknowledge Jill Lublin whose belief in help made it possible to touch so many lives; her book *Guerrilla Publicity* has been a bible for me. Dotti Albertine, thank you for your talent, being supportive and being a good friend. I want to acknowledge Irwin Zucker, founder of the Book Publicists of Southern California and to that organization for awarding *Kate's Journey* the Irwin (Industry Recognized Writers in the News) award for the Most Inspirational Book Campaign, 2003.

I wish to thank the Samuel P. Mandell Foundation for all their generous assistance and support. I am grateful to have been a part of the American Heart Association (AHA) meeting many wonderful staff members and volunteers across the country. To the division of AHA, the American Stroke Association, thank you. Emily Springer, you are not only great to work with, but I consider you a friend. Debbie McGill, thank you. To every stroke survivor who has touched my life, thank you.

Many thanks to the Progressive Taekwondo and Budo Alliance for their graciousness in awarding me an Honorary Black Belt in Taekwondo.

To Pacific Physical Therapy, Manhattan Beach, CA, especially Patty Brown, thanks for the "tune-ups" and great laughs.

To my many friends as far away as England, New Zealand and Australia, thank you. To my friends in Los Angeles, Sara Brown, Terry Anfuso, Irish Dave Black, Cathy Constant (my shopping buddy who just moved back East) Bridgid Kwan, and Kathy Murphy.

Thanks to the following for their help with *Kate's Journey:* Philip Rebentish, Leelee Loney, Mimi Lioe, Nila Campos, Steve and Debbie Ward who have stood by me in tough times, and good times, Marguerite and P. J., Debbie Shepherd and for everyone who has blessed my life. To David Abrams, one of my best friends, whose advice and assistance has helped me re-establish my life.

To God, thank you for giving me a miracle and working through me to help others.

KATE ADAMSON

Foreword

THE PONS IS THE NEUROANATOMICAL TERM FOR BRIDGE—a part of the brainstem connecting the brain with the outside world. All the traffic coming in that allows us to feel. All the traffic out that allows us to speak and move.

When Kate was thirty-three years old, in the full bloom of health, youth and life, this bridge was abruptly blown away. She suffered a pontine stroke and was paralyzed from head to toe. Suddenly, helpless and alone . . . An independent spirit now caged . . . A healthy body withered to skin and bones.

This is the story of Kate's slow, arduous, but courageous journey, from despair to hope to recovery. It takes unbelievable strength and determination, first to survive, then to let go, change, adapt, and finally to thrive. Along the way, Kate remembers the voices of belief, encouragement and faith that helped her build her own bridge to recovery. Voices of her own. Voices of others.

Kate's left arm remains paralyzed, walking is still a major effort, depression is a frequent contender, but she reaches out to others. She founded a support group for stroke survivors like herself. She began to speak on behalf of stroke survivors in national forums. Now in this book, she offers information and insights, encouragement and hope.

I first met Kate in Los Angeles, California at Rancho Los Amigos National Rehabilitation Center in 1996. On several occasions I have been a guest speaker at the "Back on Track" support group that she founded in Redondo Beach, California. It has truly been an honor and inspiration to know Kate and to share a small part of her life's work.

HELENA CHUI, M.D.
McCarron Professor of Neurology, University of Southern California Keck School of Medicine;
Associate Medical Director for Neurorehabilitation, Rancho Los Amigos National Rehabilitation Center

Introduction

I have written my story to encourage and give hope to anyone who has faced, or is facing adversity. I hope reading this book will also help those who know someone who has been down this road and can give a little insight, so that the reader can offer some relief to those who suffer. Don't get discouraged. There is hope. Adversity can strike any of us at any time and still be turned back.

In 1995, I was thirty-three years old and at the top of my game, I was a mum of two small children and never dreamed something terrible was going to happen to me. How could it? I was in the prime of my life. Then, without an invitation, a stranger came visiting. A tiny blood vessel burst and suddenly and unexpectedly I was suffering a brainstem stroke. I bled a thumbnail's worth of blood, but it paralyzed my entire body. Although capable of conscious thought, I was left unable to communicate with the world. My eyes could see but not blink. My mind could think but my voice was mute. My body was still and frozen. As God had tested Job in the Bible, God was testing me. During those long, grueling seventy days in ICU, followed by three months in rehabilitation, I didn't know if I was going to make it out of there. My faith, determination and support system kept me going.

Writing *Kate's Journey* has been a deeply moving experience. It required me to re-live the whole nightmare. I know what it's like to be kept alive by machines and to be treated like a vegetable. I know how much grace can fill the human heart in the greatest of despair. I was a body attached to a device, a consciousness trapped in a lifeless body, unable to communicate with the outside world, screaming to get out. I have fought my way back from total immobility to a joyful new life.

The lessons I have learned taught me to rise above my suffering, walk through my fear and continue to live my life (exactly as the hand is dealt). I know what it feels like to be hooked up to a respirator and not able to breathe on my own. Prior to my stroke I had taken so much in life for granted; now, I could not even take for granted my next breath.

Physically I have reached a recovery plateau. I am still paralyzed on my left side with limited use of my left leg and no use of my left arm and hand at all. However, *I am alive,* and grateful. Once again I can participate in life! Even with the paralysis of my left side, I can do many of the things today that I thought weren't possible when I first suffered the stroke. I hope my story gives others inspiration. An estimated 700,000 people suffer strokes each year. A stroke impacts not just the victims but also their families and friends. Hopefully my book will provide information and inspiration to both the stroke survivors and to their loved ones. Join me as I take you on my journey.

There are times in this book when it may seem that this is a sad or depressing story. That is anything but true. This book is the story of the triumph of the human spirit over some of the worst physical challenges that nature could test the spirit with. Many of us hope for easy lives and comfortable pleasures, but often the price for such a life is a weak spirit, a hollow soul, that counts for little in the greater scheme of life. I did not choose to be extraordinary. In 1995 I was an ordinary woman. I had little knowledge of myself or how strong I could be, or how magnificent other people could be. This is not just my struggle but, that of perhaps thousands of ordinary people who also chose to be extraordinary. Mine is a story of the power of prayer, faith and courage.

For a time my stroke knocked out my entire physical body. I was isolated and suffered from *Locked-in Syndrome,* which essentially severed all the sensory connections to my body. I have chosen the literary device of placing my thoughts in italics, so that the reader can easily tell when I am thinking thoughts locked away and buried deep inside my trapped mind. One of my greatest triumphs was to unlock my thoughts and share them with others who loved me and ultimately to use my thoughts and words to inspire and give hope to many. From my suffering, my speaking career was born. I have had the chance to touch many lives and have been inspired with a new life purpose. I can say as few people can say from their own experience, 'Every life makes a difference.'

So I invite you to share my journey, and in doing so, I hope to show that you can rise above your own problems. I hope that reading this book will put each of you in touch with just how special you are and how each of you has a real opportunity to make a difference in life. I hope you are elevated by my journey and that you get to choose your own special journey, a journey that turns weak spirits into solid strong souls.

May God Bless,
Kate's Journey

Rachael, 18 months / Stephanie, 3 years

Prologue

I AM DEAD! Not the first one to be dead. It's not shiny for me or bright. No past lives go rushing by, no present life comes before my eyes. I am Death. No one waits for me at the end of a tunnel. This is not like other people's near death experiences; their hearts stopped sending them down a path towards the light. My heart is fine beating away but its beat is killing my brain. My brain is dying. My microprocessor is being fried. The wiring is burning away at the speed of light. My brain has started to decerebrate. I am locked rigid in a fetal position going out just as I came in. I am a thirty-three-year-old fetus. This is hopeless! This is loud, chaotic and fearful. I know little, but I know I am dying. I know my precious children are terrified. I am terrified. Thoughts of my precious children occupy my dying brain cells. I hear Stephanie pounding on the door of the ambulance, "Give me back my mommy, you can't take her. I want my mom." The paramedics are helpless to comply.

Death is in the air.

Death stands near me. I can smell it, hear and touch it. I don't know if death can give mommy back any more than the paramedics can. No matter how hard I try, no matter how hard Stephanie pounds on the ambulance door screaming, death is not obliged to answer. Death is along for the ride. All of us can do no more than watch, hope and pray. The paramedics have transported death on many trips. It is no stranger to these men who have my life in their hands. They know they can do nothing but they will try to do everything. They have seen death too. Fear hangs upon us all. I am death now. There is no time for bedside manners. No one cares if I am alarmed. "We are losing her," they cry. No time to reach UCLA which is the best place for a stroke victim. The chance to receive cutting edge treatment is gone. My vital signs allow no choices; the ambulance is headed to the nearest hospital. A good hospital, but small, no MRI, no chance anyone will figure out in time what is happening to me. My first best chance is gone. The first trick is over and death has won.

The paramedics are not even sure if they should play a trump card. Should they go to sirens or just allow this dead woman to die? They think hard, they think long. In the end my age makes it impossible to just let me go peacefully into the night. I intend to rage and then rage some more against the dying of the light. I will not welcome death, I will not name it, not invite it, nor acknowledge it, but it has my attention. All the fear in the world is in my very heart that pumps away so strongly and with each pump it sends blood through a leaking artery to kill more and more brain cells. So here we go. Sirens and lights and all the speed that man can manage.

I had lived my life by a day planner and I can see it in big bold ink. "Thursday 11am-1pm funeral and 1pm-2pm eternity." Is it okay for me to survive? Won't I throw my day planner off schedule screwing up all my mourner's plans to boot? Things are falling away from me at the speed of light. I cannot feel, talk, or move my arms or legs. I can see and hear everything going on around me. I cannot breathe. I cannot make any kind of link whatsoever with my body. I am here somewhere, but where? I have no body anymore. Not one I can access. I cannot move any part of my body, not even the simplest movements. I have jangled and confused information coming in from the outside except for the unbearable pain, which is clear as crystal. I have no information I can send out to communicate with anyone. I am moving somewhere, moving so very fast. Where am I going? Where have you all gone? I should be terrified but not even that message can enter this place, my switchboard. The cells in my midbrain that route all communication with my brain are flooded with blood. They are drowning in blood, dying. Here in this place, the pons area, there is no backup system, no two sides to this part of the brain. We are closing down. My head is being severed literally and truly from my body. Oh God where am I? Where have I gone? Oh, I see a sign ahead it reads: Eternity.

Eternity is undecided about me. It can bring me relief from my pain, perhaps even peace, it can do almost anything, but it cannot end. It will last forever and even some more time after that. There is no time here in this place but there is pain, thus becoming the clock and the clock that never ends. Who is here in this place? Is it me? Do I exist? Is God here with me? Constant thoughts run through my mind. I do exist. I must exist. I feel the pain. Where are you God? How could He let this happen? Show yourself now Lord for I can tell no one. I will keep your mystery to myself, I promise. I need to see you, to touch you. Please help me. I am alone with you. In this place I can do nothing but pray. If only God could drop me a rope so I can climb up out of this pit, but I have no use of my legs and hands to hold onto the rope. I am hopeless again. There it is a tiny spark—maybe it's just a bit brighter now. Maybe I can grow legs, arms and hands. Maybe God could lasso me gently pulling me out on His own. That would be fine with me. God, it's just you and me. I want so much for this to just end. Please give me a miracle. I would do anything to have that miracle, anything but to leave my children behind. So I keep on going. I'm not going to quit. As long as there is a spark I will fan it and I will hope.

I have all the time in the world to pray. Praying is the only comfort I have. "This is only for a season," friends tell me. Why is God putting me through this? What are His plans? Life goes *on around me. Days pass, weeks with them; and I still have more and more time. I have no signal in and no signal out. I am dead. There is not a doubt about that. I know about another empty tomb and who can say that this tomb I am in won't swing outward any moment now. I may live again. It is very possible because I have hope and a flame to warm me. Yes, it is very possible that from my death I will be reborn. I may never be the same again; but I could be different. I don't want to die. Before I was death, I was Katie, mum or Mrs. Klugman to so many. I will never be those people but I may be a person again. Please God, let me live. I can see the flame now; it's making me warm. I remember Kate Adamson, a light coming to Earth to shine in a place called New Zealand. I wonder who I will be now? Will I rise up and soar upon the wings of an eagle?*

CHAPTER ONE

My New Zealand Upbringing and Early Adulthood

I was raised in New Zealand. My parents, June and Robin, met in a small town called Alexander in Central Otago on the South Island. Dad was doing some temporary work on a fruit orchard. Mum had just returned from England where she had been on a marching tour with a team called Blair Atholl. The team was now back in Alexander for a local marching exhibition. As the story goes, Dad knew one of the girls from the team and was at a dance with her one evening. There he was introduced to Mum and the rest is history!

My parents started married life on a sheep farm in a rural area of the South Island. Dad was a shepherd and Mum cooked for the farm hands. Mum stayed home to raise four children under the age of five. I have three siblings, two older brothers, Tony and Rodney, and a twin sister Lynn. My sister and I are six hours apart; we are fraternal twins, not identical. Recently, I asked Mum if she knew she was having twins when she was pregnant with us. She replied, "I learned about it only six weeks before you were born. I remember one evening I had gone to visit my doctor. He told me he could hear two hearts beating. Excitedly, I went home to tell your dad the news. He met me as I was pulling the car into the garage. When I told him the news, he collapsed against the car. "How are we going to manage four kids under the age of five?" he asked. Mum replied, "It will be fine; we'll manage."

When I was two years old, my parents moved to the city of Dunedin and built the home they are still in today, some 40 years later. Dunedin is one of the largest cities in New Zealand with a population of approximately 180,000. It is known as the Scottish City. The people are friendly and always willing to help. Dunedin is a beautiful city surrounded by lush green, hilly suburbs. The houses have tile roofs and large backyard vegetable gardens.

I lived a contented childhood and recall many cherished memories. I love to reflect back on Mum picking wonderful, succulent vegetables from the garden, which I knew would be for the evening meal. Nothing tasted better than fresh homegrown vegetables! Mum worked part-time three days a week in a yarn shop to bring in some extra money. My siblings and I went to my grandmother's home every afternoon until our parents picked us up. It was hard for my parents to manage the care of so many young children. Once we were all in school, things eased up. Dad returned to his original trade as a furniture polisher and opened a business called Hi-Glo Polishing.

On Wednesdays, my mother was home baking, filling the cake tins with tasty goodies and the house with mouth-watering smells. After school we regularly brought friends home who loved my Mum's baking. They wished their mothers could bake like my Mum! She was a wonderful cook, making jam and preserves to save money. I have happy recollections of seeing Mum sitting at the kitchen window stirring a huge pot of jam.

At the age of six Mum enrolled me in speech lessons with a woman named Miss Lawrence. She was heavyset, with strawberry-colored hair pulled up and held in place with some hairpins. She looked perpetually untidy, although she was compassionate about her teachings. Mum had heard she was a good teacher and wanted us all to take lessons. Eventually all my siblings took lessons.

At the advice of Miss Lawrence, Tony, my older brother, began some competition work. Miss Lawrence taught at a small studio in town or at her house in the suburbs. Her studio was located in the heart of town. The area is known as the Octagon, surrounded by green, leafy trees. From the window of the studio you could see a statue of the famous poet, Robbie Burns.

We were all raised with speech lessons, elocution as it was called then. The lessons were about more than just speaking; Miss Lawrence also taught us drama. Our school holidays were taken up with competition work. On countless nights I remember Mum sitting by the heater outlet in the hallway listening to us rehearse our lines. One by one each of us went into the hallway to rehearse.

A favorite piece I chose to perform was "Topsy" from *Uncle Tom's Cabin*. At competition time Mum would rub a theatrical black stick on my face and hands, giving my complexion a dark color. Afterward she washed it off with cold cream, soap and water. Mum did my hair in rags. In those days we did not even know the meaning of the word racism. I loved being on stage and becoming the character I was portraying. "I'm going to become an actress one day," I told myself. My sister Lynn invariably got stage fright when it was her turn to go on. Mum would push me on first without a moment to think about it. All of a sudden I would look out into the audience and hundreds of faces were staring at me. The stage lights shone brightly in my eyes. I had butterflies in my stomach for the first few minutes. I remembered what my speech teacher told me, "Take deep breaths, Kate. Concentrate on one word at a time." I would open my mouth and a steady flow of words came out. I felt charismatic being on stage.

All the hard work paid off. We all came home with medals and cups from the speech competitions. I felt my life up to this point was about school and speech lessons. As I approached my teens, I felt confused about what I wanted out of life. I found having fun with my friends was more important to me than academic achievement, yet I always seemed to have this gift for language and drama. However, I constantly caused my parents sleepless nights.

At 19, I was feeling restless and uncomfortable in my own skin. One New Year's Eve, in 1980, I met an American, and fell in love as only a 19-year-old can. I found true love and he was the one! He asked me to go to the United States with him. I don't know what I was thinking, maybe that I'd ride off into the sunset and live happily ever after. Being headstrong, I thought I knew what was best for me and I decided to see the world. Unfortunately, as I have found out, life doesn't work the way we demand it to. I left problems behind, but found out we only gain a new set of problems, every time we change partners or grab a new chair to sit in. Life is a journey from which we learn, with or without our own consent.

My parents were against my leaving New Zealand, but I was determined to go. I had never flown in a plane, or even been to the North Island of New Zealand, but I was sure I knew what was best for me. At 19, all distances seemed short and all obstacles surmountable. As someone later said, "On the wings of youth, I flew into the unknown."

My journey took me from New Zealand to Los Angeles, California in the United States—from the United States to London—and two years later from London back to Los Angeles. In case things didn't work out, I had a plan B, which was to be an au pair in London. After spending several weeks in America, fate chose plan B. (I knew in my heart the man I thought was Mr. Right was not the man I wanted to marry. He did not even turn out to be Mr. Rogers let alone Mr. Right.)

I was excited about the family I would be living with in London. From the details the nanny agency had given me in New Zealand about the family, I was ecstatic. I would have my own room with a TV and the use of a car. It all sounded so perfect. I imagined Robert Young and Donna Reed to be my new employers and that I would be taking care of the children from "Mary Poppins."

I arrived after a long flight at Heathrow Airport in London to find my new family waiting for me holding a large sign reading "Adamson." We picked up my baggage and drove on the autobahn to their suburb. Susan, the mother helped to settle me into my new room. "Would you like some supper?" she asked. "Oh, no thanks, I'm not hungry," I said politely. I realized after she had left, that supper in England meant dinner. In New Zealand we called that "tea-time" and I soon realized that I had to pick up on the different cultural sayings and slang. *I was in a different country now.* I went to bed that evening starving. I was too shy to ask for something to eat.

The nanny job lasted three months. It wasn't what I thought it was going to be. The two children were brats, and the wonderful perks I thought I was going to have, didn't happen. I hated living there! The house was situated in the path of airplane traffic, and every three minutes I would hear the noise of planes flying overhead, causing the house to vibrate. On a daily basis Susan had a long "to do" list prepared to keep me busy all day. I had the use of the car only to take the children to school and home. My bedroom that I had dreamed about was a small room with a hardwood floor and a tiny black and white TV in the corner. Not only was I expected to be the nanny to the children, I had to prepare the family meals and clean up after them. This was particularly hard because I didn't know a thing about cooking, but Susan soon changed that. I was only allowed to eat with the children at their mealtime, which was also hard.

I remember when the London family planned their summer vacation to Greece. I was excited about going along as the nanny, until Susan explained to me that I wouldn't be going. I was to stay home and keep an eye on things and I wouldn't be getting paid for that week either. *This job wasn't what I had imagined.* I did get on well with the husband who had a wonderful sense of humor and would often tell jokes. Then one night Susan came to my room and told me to be seen and not heard. That was the final straw for me. *Me! Seen and not heard?* In retrospect, could it have been that Robert Young was looking for Lolita? Or perhaps Donna Reed was just paranoid or jealous as a hen. Looking back, I don't know how I lasted three months.

I had another nanny friend named Jean. She was from Australia and was having problems with her family. Both of us had decided to leave our families and go into London looking for work. "Where will we live Jean?" I asked her, concerned. "Don't worry, let's get out of here and take it one step at a time," she said optimistically. While my host family slept, I spent the night quietly packing my things, ready to leave the next morning. My heart was racing in anticipation and nervousness. The next day I did my usual morning duties, taking the kids to school and waited until the parents left for work. Susan handed me a list; her mother-in-law was coming to stay and she wanted things in order. I felt like a run-away slave on the Underground Railroad.

Mid-morning I heard the honk of a taxicab. I briskly grabbed my suitcase and hurried outside. I breathed a sigh of relief as I sat in the car while the driver put my suitcase in the trunk. *Wow! I did it! I can't believe I'm doing this? Free, free, free at last!* As the taxicab pulled out of the driveway I remember thinking, *Okay God, I'm in your hands now.* As I was leaving, Susan drove up in her car with her mother-in-law. When she saw the taxicab driving off, she started running after the vehicle screaming, "You can't do this to me, I need help. You can't do this!" I glanced back knowing I had made the right decision. "Just keep driving," I told the cab driver.

Jean and I walked into a posh fish-and-chips restaurant called Flanagans. The manager had us fill out an application and asked our experience in the restaurant business. The most experience I had at that point in my life was carrying my dirty dishes from the kitchen table across to the kitchen counter! *How hard could this be?*

The manager hired both of us, and I immediately enjoyed my new adventure. I took to the job like a duck takes to water. I loved being around people and letting my personality shine through. I spent two years in London, traveling and working at the restaurant. Jean and I had found a suburb that housed Australians and New Zealanders. I was having the time of my life. (I also worked at El Vino's wine bar; my co-workers and I stay in touch to this present day. Their memories of me are of the "goodtime girl" always ready to party, shop, and have a laugh.) I had made many friends and was able to support myself. However, as much as I liked London, I did not see myself putting down roots. My passport was running out and I decided to return to New Zealand.

On my way back to New Zealand, I visited some friends in Los Angeles, whom I had met on my first visit there two years earlier. I stayed six weeks, basking in the sun of sunny Palm Springs. I could not imagine how life could get any better and decided that I would move to L.A. instead of returning to New Zealand. I immediately started looking for a restaurant job, since I had only $300 in my pocket. My ticket back home had been canceled with no refund. *I have to make it now,* I thought. I kept remembering all of the movies I had seen about the small town girl making good in the big city. No matter what, I was determined to make it. I struggled to support myself as a waitress. It was during this time that I met my first husband, Duncan. He was living in California, originally a mid-west guy from Kansas City. Duncan was in the Real Estate business. We dated for a couple of years and got married in Las Vegas. After that, I continued my waitress job but I felt in my heart I wanted more. I loved people and wanted to look for a "people job."

Another waitress at the Velvet Turtle was a Mary Kay consultant. She would talk about her sales meetings and the prizes she was winning while making money at the same time. *I can do that,* I thought, *I love makeup and I'd be working around people.* I went to one of the sales meetings and signed on right away as a Mary Kay beauty consultant. I carried my pink bags everywhere I went and stored the inventory in my home. I had business cards made up and made a point of handing out five cards a day. I enjoyed my new career, and I loved meeting new friends and helping them grow. I went on to become a director, calling my team, "The Down Under Wonders." I went everywhere with my pink bags and my free car. My sales meetings required me to drive the freeways, which was a challenge for a New Zealand gal like me. I had never driven on a freeway but I knew the only way to face my fear was to do it. Back home I was used to driving on the other side of the road. Gradually, the more I drove the freeways the easier it became.

The marriage with Duncan lasted only four years. Today we are good friends. With the breakup of the marriage, I had to keep selling Mary Kay products. It was hard to stay focused during this emotional period. I had to sell a lot of lipsticks and cleansers just to keep the car. I found everything overwhelming—recruiting new consultants and keeping my business going while dealing with the divorce at the same time. I decided not to stay with the Mary Kay business and went back to working in the restaurant business. My Mary Kay career taught me a lot, and today I still have friends who have remained in the profession.

I met my second husband, Steven, in 1990. Steven was a personal injury attorney, practicing in Century City. We met through a mutual friend. We had fun being friends and going places. I found myself spending more and more time with him. In 1991 we were married. Thirteen days after the marriage, I was pregnant with our first child. I took a trip home to New Zealand while in the early stages of my pregnancy. Steven did not come with me, and since my parents were not in the states for the wedding, they were eager to hear all about him. The man I had just married was fifteen years my senior. All my parents wanted was for me to be happy.

CHAPTER TWO

Hello Darkness
My Old Friend

*I*came back to the States from my trip to New Zealand. I was hoping that being married and having a beautiful baby on the way would finally result in my parents' approval. It did not. To my parents I guess I will always be the little girl who ran away at nineteen. The acceptance I longed so deeply for was not to be found in New Zealand.

I had a horrendous labor giving birth to my first child, Stephanie. Four days of labor and no results. I was finally given an emergency Cesarean section and gave birth to a healthy eight-pound baby. I was ecstatic to join the ranks of motherhood. I found myself back in the gym working out six weeks after the birth. I had always been a health nut and physical fitness meant a lot. As soon as my gynecologist gave me the clearance, I was at the fitness center again. I was placed on a very low dosage birth control pill that had minimum side effects.

After the birth of Stephanie, I started experiencing some migraine headaches and also started losing weight. I began having symptoms of my hair falling out and some nervousness. I was referred to an endocrinologist who ran some tests, ran a blood panel and an ultrasound on my thyroid. My thyroid gland had completely shut down and I was about to be put on medication when three months later the gland went back to working on its own. I needed no medication.

In December of 1993, I was ready for the birth of our second daughter, Rachel. Because of previous complications my doctor scheduled another Cesarean. I knew ahead of time what was in store for me. On the 16th of December, Rachel Elizabeth Klugman joined our little family. This beautiful tiny baby weighed no more than six pounds with the most delicate features. *What a wonderful Christmas gift!*

The recovery process from the surgery was a breeze. I knew what to expect and bounced back quickly. Again I waited for clearance from my doctor and went back on birth control. The same thyroid process I had experienced after Stephanie's birth started happening immediately after giving birth to Rachel. My thyroid gland once again returned to normal working function three months later. Tests previously ran showed I had developed a rare and silent thyroid condition called Thyroiditis.

When Rachel was 17 months old, the migraines started again. I didn't panic. I naturally assumed it was my thyroid condition and I began to tolerate the headaches. I did what had worked for me in the past; I would lie down in a dark quiet room with a cold compress on my head. I had massages and took long relaxing baths. The pain lessened a little. Somehow I continued about my daily activities trying to block the pain out and focus on being a wife and mother.

Keeping a house is like threading beads on a string with no knot at the end. I was continuously keeping a "to-do" list in spite of how I felt. *I'll feel better soon*, I told myself. I relied on many of my friends to help me with the girls so I could rest and relieve the pain. In mid-June, I satisfied my husband's constant requests to get medical attention by going to see a chiropractor. My husband wanted me to see my private medical doctor but I felt he was too far away to drive to. I made the fateful decision to seek help from a chiropractor instead of a trained medical doctor. This choice will haunt me for the rest of my life. *Maybe this will help. I just want some relief.* The chiropractor's treatments did not help. In fact, my headaches became worse. I began to just tolerate the pain. The chiropractor did not diagnose that I was having a stroke.

There was not a cloud on the horizon. Everything seemed fine except I was experiencing these bad migraines. I was no stranger to headaches. I saw this wonderful month of June through a heavy gloss of pain. I found it hard to participate in the normal events of my life. At times my head felt like it was going to explode. The pain was unbearable. I just cried and cried. In the mornings I felt some slight relief. I was really talking myself into feeling better. I continued with my daily routine of exercise that made me feel better. It was also a time for reflection. *I know it will get better, I just need to be patient. God guide me through this.*

On June 28, I made a commitment to a girlfriend to work out at her gym. *I can't let her down. I'll just try my best to work through this.* I woke up that morning with a dull headache. Despite how I felt, I decided to meet her. *Maybe my workout will relieve this. Besides it will take my mind off things.* The children went into the "kids club" while we worked out. My lingering headache proceeded to gradually get worse. I decided not to push a strenuous workout and did a little walking on the treadmill before gathering my daughters and going home.

That afternoon Stephanie had a birthday party to attend. I was relieved I could drop her off and go home to lie down. *I think a nap will help me feel better.* Before picking Stephanie up, I stopped for coffee. I ran into a couple of gym buddies who asked if I was feeling okay. I must have looked like I was in pain. I chatted briefly before leaving to get my daughter.

Wednesday evenings I normally went to my regular small church group, but this Wednesday I didn't feel well enough to go. My headache was getting worse and worse. "Go ahead without me, I'm going to bed early to shake this headache," I said. My husband left with both girls leaving me to relax. *A nice long bubble bath sounds good.* Before going upstairs I phoned my girlfriend, Cherri and told her how awful I was feeling. "This is the worse headache I have ever had, Cherri. I think I'll just go to bed.

I'll see you tomorrow," I said We made plans to meet at the mall for a puppet show in the morning. "Okay, Kate, get some rest. You have been experiencing these headaches for a while, I think you should call your doctor," she said concerned. I hung up the phone, *She's right, I need to call my doctor tomorrow and look into these annoying headaches. This has gone on too long.*

Soaking in the tub felt heavenly. I just wished the pain would go away. I cried tears into the washcloth. Before climbing into bed, I took a mild sleeping pill. *I hope I feel better in the morning.* I drifted off into a deep sleep.

My alarm went off at six that next morning. I got out of bed, walked into my bathroom and started running the water for a shower. I had a lot of work ahead of me and I was anxious to get things ready. With Rachel still in diapers, I needed to prepare a diaper bag and snacks. As I was showering and lathering shampoo into my hair, I noticed I still had a dull, lingering headache. Waves of dizziness swept over me. *I'll probably feel better after I eat something. Getting some rest would have helped this.*

I stepped out of the shower, putting my pajamas on so I could dry my hair. As I slipped on my pajama bottoms, I felt my left side start to give way under me. It felt like my muscles had gone like jelly. I had no strength to stand up. A painless feeling swept throughout my body. I reached out to steady myself against the counter. *That's odd. I think I had better sit down for a minute.* The sensation startled me. I sat on the marble ledge surrounding my bathtub. *This doesn't seem normal. I think I had better lie down in bed. Perhaps I'm coming down with something.*

Grabbing my pajama top, I cautiously walked into my bedroom and flopped down onto the bed. I glanced over at my husband sleeping soundly. "Wake up, I don't feel well," I said gently nudging him. He made a few groaning sounds and rolled over onto his other side. I tried to conceal my fear and once again said, "I need you to wake up." He immediately sat up in bed, "What's wrong? Is it one of the kids?"

"Something is wrong. I don't feel well," I told him. In a groggy voice he said, "Let me go back to sleep, I'll drive you to see the doctor later." He lay back down pulling the covers over him. "No, I think I need help now," I said panicking. Steven got up and went over to the phone. He dialed the neighbors. *I know you like to sleep in, but I'm scared. Something is terribly wrong.* "Hi Rocky, would you mind coming over and helping with the kids? Kate isn't feeling well and I need to take her to the doctor." There was a brief silence and he hung up the phone. "Okay, Rocky is on his way over," he said. *On his way over! I need to button my pajama top up.*

I attempted to button my top. *What's happening? My left arm won't move?* Frustrated, I screamed out. A stream of slurred sounds came out. *What's happening? Why can't I speak properly? Can't you understand me? I need help now! What's Rocky going to do?* I saw a look of disbelief on my husband's face. "Honey, don't worry. I'm getting help." The doorbell rang and he hurried to let Rocky in. I could hear them talking. Rocky came into the bedroom and looking at me hastily said, "Dial 911 immediately." *My God! What is happening to me! Help!*

I heard the sound of sirens and within moments an ambulance was at my house. Heavy footsteps of men running up the stairs could be heard. "In here," shouted Steven alarmed. The paramedics quickly assembled a stretcher and cautiously eased me onto it. Rocky and my husband stood back, their faces expressing concern. *I don't want to be sick! Please God don't let there be anything wrong!*

I remember thinking as the ambulance attendants were carefully taking me downstairs, *Why are they making a big deal about this? I can walk down these stairs.* Little did I know that I would never walk normally without a brace and a very noticeable limp. Unknown to me, my legs were paralyzed. With all the confusion, Stephanie and Rachel were standing with Rocky's wife at the bottom of the stairs. "What's wrong with mommy?"

Stephanie asked. Rachel was in Doreen's arms crying. *I'll be home before the end of the day. My babies! My babies!*

I could read the expression on Stephanie's face, "Where is mommy going?" I'll never forget her look as I was carted away on the stretcher and placed into the ambulance. Neighbors gathered outside their houses to watch. I suddenly became very frightened inside, *What is going to happen?* The ambulance attendant reached for an oxygen mask. "It's okay. I just need to give you some oxygen. Try to take some deep breaths." I followed his instructions wishing this wasn't happening, whatever it was. I knew inside the deepest part of my soul that this wasn't good. *Hello darkness my old friend. I've come to visit you again. Are you there?*

In the emergency room, I was disoriented. The darkness was my only friend. I could hear people talking, but I couldn't respond. *Please somebody help! I'm frightened! What's happening to me? Why can't I say what I am thinking?*

The ER doctor found it hard to believe I might be having a stroke. "She's so young and healthy," he told my husband. The doctors didn't know what was happening. In an act of caution, the doctor hooked me up to a respirator. This meant I had to be intubated. Tubes had to go down my nose to my lungs. This was a horrible, difficult and painful procedure. The procedure lowered my blood pressure, slowing down my bleeding. I was in a world where a tenth of a second and a millimeter of space made the difference between life and death. With my normal blood pressure, I would have bled to death in minutes. The doctor, groping for a cause, attempted a CT (Computerized Tomogram) scan of my brain. Although making conventional sense, he was looking for the cause in entirely the wrong place. That's like looking for Yellowstone National Park in New York!

The CT scan results appeared to be normal so the doctor took me off the respirator pulling the tube out of my lungs, through my nose and attempting to waken me. I could hear this voice and feel him gently nudging me. "Kate, wake up if you can hear me. Do you know your name? How many children do you have? Are you hearing me?" I heard him all right, but to my horror, I could do nothing to communicate. His attempts at waking me were unsuccessful and although I could hear the voices, my eyes remained closed. I had been given a number of medications, including morphine. The doctors became worried that I was over responding to the medication.

Where are my pajamas? How did I get in this hospital gown? What's happening! Oh God, please help me!

When I was taken off the respirator, my metabolism sped up which increased the rate of my internal bleeding. Instead of waking up, I went into a rigid fetal position. The doctor suddenly became concerned and decided to treat my case as if I was having a major bleeding incident. He told my husband he was in fear that I was bleeding to death in front of his eyes. *God let this be over soon! Was that severe headache last night a warning sign that something was about to happen? Why didn't I pay more attention to the headaches?* (I still, to this day, have the memory of the suffering, the crunching sound of cartilage in my nose breaking as the tubes went in and out.) Three trips to hell for the price of one.

Steven had a conversation with my private doctor whom I should have driven to see instead of a chiropractor. The doctor advised him to instruct the hospital doctors to look in my brain stem for a possible stroke. With a lawyer looking over their shoulders, the hospital doctors were afraid not to conduct the tests. Precious moments that meant so much to my recovery had been lost in a vain search to find a needle in a haystack. The latest medical technology was slipping beyond my reach. The medical miracles of the last twenty years weren't any use for me. My youth and overall health worked against me in this case making the obvious hard to see. (When a bill finally came for the ER room, it was over $96,000. For that I was kept alive, but no one could determine why I was sick.)

The hospital where I was did not have a MRI (Magnetic Resonance Imaging machine). If my private physician was right, the only way to know for sure if I was having a stroke was for me to have a MRI. I was therefore transferred by ambulance to Torrance Memorial Hospital as quickly as arrangements could be made.

The ER doctor called the on-call neurologist, Dr. Kneisley, who took over my case. The transfer in the ambulance was a blur. I remember going in and out of consciousness. By the time I reached Torrance Memorial my body was continuously having convulsions. Upon being admitted to Torrance, I vomited and was suddenly foaming at the mouth. *Where am I? What's happening?* Suddenly, I found myself slowly moving into a machine. I could hear the voice of someone saying, "Try to lie still and relax. We have several sets of tests. Just try to lie still. In a moment you'll be hearing some noises." *I'm scared! What's happening to me?*

All of a sudden, I stopped moving. It was still. There was silence until slowly I heard what sounded like the beating of a drum, gradually getting louder and faster. Bang! Bang! Bang! No matter how much I tried to lie motionless. I couldn't. *I feel claustrophobic inside here. I just want out of here! I feel like I can't breathe.* My body kept going into spasms, making it impossible to get a clear MRI reading. Everything after this was a blur. I remember nothing for what seemed a lifetime. Many things would change. One thing remained constant: my husband would be the bridge between me and the world that existed outside my body.

I was admitted to the ICU for observation. Blue mittens were placed on my hands to prevent me from pulling any tube or IVs out. The following morning, the doctor felt I looked clinically the same. I lay there looking up at the doctor and my husband. "It's hard to tell if she can understand us. I think she can hear us," the doctor said. *Yes! I can hear you. I can't move or speak, but I hear you. God, I have to be able to communicate somehow.* My husband refused to believe I was dying but the doctor offered little hope.

Dr. Kneisley, a neurologist, ordered some chest X-rays and followed my care closely. I recall waking up and lying on something flat, hard and cold. *What's happening now?* Steven wanted some drugs administered to me that would lessen the swelling in my brain. "You have to treat this as if she's had a stroke," he told the doctor. The neurologist refused, explaining he couldn't do that until they were sure what was wrong. Steven asked the doctor what would happen if I had a brain tumor and the doctor told him I would die within a few months. So, Steven once again insisted that the doctor treat me for a stroke since by assuming that I had a stroke and not a tumor, some good could be done. The doctor refused my husband's request and a day passed before the anti-inflammatory treatment was administered. The doctor recommended and ordered an emergency vertebral angiogram to determine if I had a brain tumor or a stroke. This had both prognostic and therapeutic implications. Because I had previously been given blood thinners, the procedure was touch-and-go. I was given a shot of Vitamin K to help speed up the clotting of my blood.

I was wheeled into the operating room on a gurney, my husband at my side. The procedure was too much for Steven and he passed out (trying his best to fall away from the operating table.) Now I was alone. My eyes looked around the room. Everything was stainless steel and clean looking. How eerie. Dr. Hoffman, a radiologist performed the angiogram. I don't remember much. I recall the surgeon leaning over and saying, "Great news, Kate. You've suffered a stroke. We found the problem. Your vertebral artery is occluded." *What is he saying? I don't understand what a stroke is? I just want to feel better. How can this be good news? I'm too groggy to care.*

Doubt had been replaced with hope, or had it? Since my husband had fainted in the operating room, he never met Dr. Hoffman. Fate placed the doctor in the elevator as Steven was riding up to my room. He heard Dr. Hoffman telling a nurse that I was the worst thing he had seen in a very long time. He said I was a tragic case and could look forward to death if I were lucky and life if I were not lucky. My husband kept this in his heart and filed it away under a mistaken belief that would be overcome by a gracious God.

Overnight, my life had been turned into a nightmare. The doctor started me on the anti-coagulation drug, Heparin. Although I was breathing spontaneously, I was unable to handle my secretions and remained intubated. I was watched very closely.

I remember another doctor came by for a consultation. She felt I needed a feeding tube placed in my stomach because of the difficulty of getting enough nourishment from my IVs. As the doctor was operating on me to put the tube in, it dawned on me: *Oh my God! I'm awake! I can feel them ripping my stomach open.* The operation lasted two or three years in my time. I was too sick and frail to be moved to the operating room. A nurse put a mouth guard in for me to bite on. *Why is she doing that? What's going to happen?* The doctor thought I was a dead woman and they did not give me adequate pain medication.

I lay there, watching what was going on around me. I could feel everything the doctor was doing and I had no way of communicating. Imagine being cut into and not being able to respond? *They haven't given me enough anesthesia! I can feel this!* I felt the whole operation, every cut. I could do nothing but lay there. I prayed it would be over soon but it seemed to last forever. *God willing, I'll get through this!*

This tube was where I would receive all my nourishment and medications. From this point on, all medications were crushed up, dissolved with a little water before being put into a syringe and passed through the tube. *How had I lived through that? How could I live through any of this?*

A lung specialist, Dr. Kolodney, was called in to monitor my breathing problems which had become severe. Out of all the doctors, he was the first to believe in my chances of recovery. He was the only one to listen to Steven. At this point all the other doctors thought Steven was insane because he refused to give up. They even noted in my medical records that Steven was delusional because he refused to believe that I would not die. Dr. Kolodney took hours to speak with Steven. They both agreed to become partners and to see to it that I had a chance to survive this awful stroke.

Dr. Kolodney's compassion, skill and belief made all the difference in the world. Without the help of a lawyer and a doctor working together, there is no doubt I would have fulfilled the expectations of the medical staff and died within days.

I was not done with tubes, not by a long shot. My husband asked Dr. Kolodney to remove the tube down my airway. This was a truly amazing suggestion. Steven was trying to prevent me from having a scar. He and the doctor could not admit how precarious and seemingly hopeless my position was. The doctor agreed but his nurse begged him not to. She felt I was desperately ill and that I would drown in my own secretions if they took the tubes out. As soon as the tubes were removed, I began to go down hill. I was rapidly drowning in my own saliva. I could not handle my secretions. I could not tolerate breathing on my own. My oxygen saturation level began to fall, requiring constant suctioning. Dr. Kolodney told Steven that I needed an emergency tracheotomy. "This will be a tiny, two-inch scar; it's a matter of life and death," he stated. Approval was given and a tracheotomy was performed July 5th. (Looking back, it is insane that the biggest worry on my care-giver's mind was me having a tiny scar.)

As horrible as the breathing tubes down my nose had been, I received little comfort from the tracheotomy. I was producing an overabundance of fluids. A vacuum device was inserted into the trachea to keep my lungs clear. Every time a respiratory therapist approached me, my body tightened, going into convulsions. I almost jumped off the bed as the mucus was sucked out of my lungs. The treatments were unbearable. *Here we go again. How can anyone put up with these treatments?* (I can still feel, in my mind, the suction treatments that kept my airway open and my lungs from filling up with fluid.) I would recover from this ordeal, only for it to begin again. At this point in my recovery, I needed the treatments every twenty minutes. *All this horror around me and I can't get the chance to rest.*

I was not being given pain medication because of the neurological problems. I had to deal with the pain, the boredom and with my friend, the darkness. *Hello my old friend. I've come to visit you again.*

Life in ICU was constant, unchanging, and full of little hope. The days dragged on and on. Seventy days would pass before I'd leave ICU. I heard nothing but the constant beeping of the machines that I was hooked up to. I could feel the feeding tube dangling from my stomach with no way of reaching down to touch it. The memories of the procedures haunted me. *I'm in the prime of my life, yet I have suffered a massive stroke.* I was completely paralyzed except for some voluntary eye movements. This condition is called "Locked-in Syndrome." I was conscious, had cognitive thinking abilities, but was unable to speak or move, and had a perfect sense of pain. I hurt everywhere but I could move nowhere. *Why should I live? How can this be called living? Why should I take my next breath? I will not give up!* The darkness was not empty. There was a strong presence there. God was with me and if God was there, I could not be without hope. I was trapped inside my body. Steven was outside, doing anything to get in, anything. I knew he would move heaven and hell to reach me.

Within hours it began, a dozen people praying for me. By week's end, thousands of people around the world, around the clock, were praying for me. Not an hour, not a minute went by when someone, somewhere was not praying for me. I could not see help but I could feel it approach. I had my faith, my husband and my children.

I'm not going to leave my children, whatever pain may come, whatever horror is around the corner. In order to stay alive, I would endure whatever treatment, no matter how dehumanizing. I will overcome any obstacle to get back to my children, I will. Home. I am going to go home. No matter what, no matter how; I am going home.

Dr. Jeffrey Saver's Comments:

Stroke is injury to the brain due to blockage or rupture of a blood vessel. The brain requires a constant flow of blood to carry oxygen and nutrients to nerve cells. Four main arteries carry blood to the brain: the right and left carotid arteries and the right and left vertebral arteries. In Kate's case, one of the vertebral arteries became blocked, cutting off blood flow to the base of the brain— the brainstem. Damage to nerve tracks passing through the brainstem disconnected the upper parts of the brain, the cerebral hemispheres, from the spinal cord and the body. Kate became "locked-in," her intact cerebral hemispheres enabling her to be awake and aware, but unable to move her limbs or facial muscles because the connections between from the cerebral hemispheres to the spinal cord were injured by the stroke.

Stroke is the third leading cause of death and the leading cause of disability in the developed world. Stroke is often thought of as a disease of the elderly. However, strokes do commonly affect middle-aged adults, young adults, and even children. Up to one-third of all strokes occur in individuals under the age of 65. The locked-in syndrome is one of the rarest and most feared consequences of a stroke.

—⚏—⚏—⚏—

PRAYER JOURNAL EXCERPTS FROM FRIENDS
AND FAMILY MEMBERS WHILE KATE WAS IN ICU:

7/5/95

Dear Kate & Steven,

I am so moved by Christ's Love for you both. I am so thankful for your lives crossing my path. I want to share Isaiah 53:5.5-6.

Surely he took up our infirmities and carried Kate's sorrows. He was pierced for our transgressions, he was bruised for our iniquities, the chastisement for our peace was upon him, and by His stripes we are healed.

By his wounds, Kate is healed. We like sheep have all gone astray, each of us has turned his own way and the Lord has laid on him the iniquity of us all. Because of those dark hours two thousands years ago, God can say to me and Kate, I will never leave you, I will never forsake Kate.

I pray God would honor his word and heal you day by day. I love you so much Kate and look forward to seeing all the wonderful things God has planned for you.

Love,
Karen Johnson

7/3/95

Kate,

I thank God for you, In Mark 5:34 Jesus spoke these words, "Daughter, your faith has made you well. Go in peace and be healed of your affliction." I pray that while God is healing you, your peace is mighty and your suffering is minute and your faith as large as the mustard tree. When God later commands you, "Little girl, I say to you, arise," you will obey and get up. I know how much God loves you, more than I could ever understand. You are in my prayers.

I love you,
Chris Kirby

7/4/95

Dear Kate,

I just wanted to say that you have been on my mind all day and in my prayers. The Lord is working and it's exciting to know He is healing you!

Sunday at church my daughter Christina and I passed Stephanie being carried up the stairs. I didn't even realize who it was until I felt a little arm reached out and touched me. When I turned around, I saw Stephanie giving me a big smile and waving. I didn't even realize she recognized me, but she certainly wanted us to know she was there. She's a special girl and God is going to give you many more years to enjoy your daughters. We love you.

Love,
Laura Warfield

7/8/95

My Dearest Friend Kate,

I miss you! You are in my heart and in my prayers. I love you, You have been such a blessing in my life. The kids are doing great! Jamie calls Stephanie on the phone and they talk. I know in my heart you will be out of here soon. I am here for you and your husband and kids. I never feel like I can do enough. We will see you through this time in your life. I know how strong you are and I know what an asset you are to all of us. The people from your church are all doing such a wonderful thing. All the prayers and all the support is awesome! You are so beautiful inside and out. May God heal you quickly and keep you in comfort.

I love you.
Cherri

7/6/95

Kate,

My beautiful sister in Christ, I am so blessed to be able to see you again today. Adam and I pray for you, and we have asked friends from all over to continue to hold you and your family up in prayer. I'm so touched by the impact you have had on so many lives. I have met so many people who have been drawn closer to Christ and have been blessed by you. We believe in the Lord for your healing, and trusting in his love. He holds you in his arms and directs your paths. He loves you with a love so great we cannot fully understand.

I love you.
Juli

7/11/95

Dear Kate,

I came by to let you know I love you!

This is temporary. I am so excited about seeing you stand up in church and giving your testimony! God is going to get the glory out of this! And you are going to be stronger and happier, and more blessed, and closer to Jesus than you have ever been. Kate, I love you. You are such a giver and you're going to reap such wonderful blessings. Thank you for reaching out to me. God Bless! I thank you for your care and sincerity. Jesus Christ is your Lord. You're a miracle!

You will be well soon, and very soon!

By Jesus Christ's stripes, you are healed totally!
Debbie Albino

7/23/95

Dearest Kate,

You are doing so very well!

I am so thrilled. I was here last Sunday, one week ago, but you were sleeping. You are making major improvements every day. Now you are moving your right hand and foot and starting your left side.

You are a strong woman, physically and spiritually, keep fighting.

"Our God is an awesome God, he reigns with power and love. Our God is an awesome God."

Kate, your mommy just arrived. (3pm) Enjoy her! Let her love you! She loves you.

Love,
Penny

7/25/95

Dear Kate,

Thanks for letting me play music for you tonight. I hope I can do it a lot, I'll pray for God's timing to get out of work and come often and play for you (violin).

You are a fighter, girl Don't lose that fire, keep working that physical therapy. Pretend you are maxing the stair stepper! And, my prayer for you is what I had to learn when I was real sick, still the thoughts, listen for God's voice, resist the enemy's lies, learn what he wants you to know right now. I believe you'll be all right and I'm praying for you.

Love,
Lisa Anders

CHAPTER THREE

In the Blink of an Eye

I felt very frightened and isolated. I remember familiar faces of friends popping in and out of ICU. Although there was a steady flow of visitors, I was alone, not able to communicate with anyone. I felt like a character in a *Twilight Zone* episode. There were moments I doubted my sanity. Sometimes I wished I had gone insane because then I could recover and this dreadful play would be over. The director would shout "cut," the camera would stop rolling, and I could get up and go home. What a lovely thought. I feared something much worse had happened to me than just losing my mind. My only companion was God. My mind bounced back and forth like a ping-pong ball between pain, loneliness and terror. I was nowhere near ready to "Be still and know that I am God."

There has to be some rational way out of this mess; no God would let this happen to me. If I could just tell someone I am alive then I could get help. No matter how hard I tried, I couldn't speak. I tried to mouth the word *home* to anyone who came near. *Don't any of you understand me? I have to be able to get home; this has to be a bad dream, I'm a good person, things like this don't happen to good people!*

Sadly, I wasn't going anywhere physically or spiritually. I was attached to IVs with a hole in my throat and a tube hanging from my stomach. Close the hole in my neck and stomach; remove the tubes. I was dead. *I have tubes everywhere. It's no use. My cries for help are useless! Who can I cry to? Who will hear me? Besides, no real tears flow and no sound comes out. It's useless!*

I noted everything. I noted nothing. I just wanted home. Steven and a friend, Rhonda, were in my room discussing concerns about Rachel. My eighteen month old was fighting an ear infection and was on medication. I listened as they spoke. *I should be handling this. Steven is such a sissy about doctors and needs me to tell him what to do. I wish I could speak right now.* He was lost trying to remember where Rachel's medication was kept. *It's in the fridge on the side self.* "Rhonda, I wonder, if we ask Kate a question can she respond?" he asked. *Yes, please ask me something!* "We could try but don't be too disappointed if nothing happens," she said trying to be kind to Steven. "Kate, I want you to blink if you understand me." Both looked anxiously into my eyes as I tried to blink.

With all my strength, I closed my eyelids and slowly opened them. *Yes, I can understand you.* "You can understand me. You can understand me," he said excitedly. "Kate, this is awesome news, praise God," Rhonda said. Not wanting Steven to be heart broken, Rhonda suggested the blink was a coincidence. "No Rhonda, I refuse to believe that. "Okay Kate, blink once for yes," he said watching me.

This was it; my whole life hinged on this one chance. *Can I find a way to blink my eyelids because I want to? I'm not sure I can do this again.* It felt like a million years had gone by and nothing I thought had become reality in the physical world. I had tried and tried to move something; say something; do something; and I failed. Praying, I asked God to help me. Struggling, I thought and concentrated hard; still nothing happened. "Come on Kate. You can do this," Steven said. *It's no use. I just can't.* I gave up and suddenly, my eyelid blinked.

I blinked my eyelids. I did it! Thank you God. "Now Kate, try blinking your eyelids twice for "no," he said holding his hands to his mouth waiting in anticipation. *This takes a lot of my energy. I hope I can do this.* Slowly, I blinked my eyelids twice. "Praise God! Praise God!" Steven said. *Praise God is*

right! Thank you God. I've made contact, now I am not alone.
Steven anxiously went to the nurses' station. "I want this docu-
mented. Kate can communicate," he said eagerly. "I want a sign
made so people are aware she can understand." Since no one
jumped to help him, he took some paper off the desk and made
his own sign. It said in large letters: **THIS IS A HUMAN BEING
LYING HERE. SHE UNDERSTANDS WHAT YOU SAY.
PLEASE TREAT HER AS A PERSON.**

The sign was taped above my bed and from that point on I
communicated by blinking my eyelids. *I'm no longer alone.
Thank you God for giving me the gift to blink my eyelids.* The
process was exhausting but I had no other way of communicating with the outside world. The nurses gave my husband a clipboard with a sheet of the alphabet attached. My blinking became
more complex. I would blink "yes" or "no" to each letter as
Steven pointed to them.

"Kate, do you have any idea what happened to you?" he
asked. I blinked "no." Steven said, "You have had a stroke."
What's that? Grabbing a piece of paper and pencil he drew a dia-
gram explaining what had happened. *Steven, I'm too sick to be
looking at diagrams.* I listened to him ramble on. *I don't have a
clue what you are saying.*

From that point on, everyone used the alphabet board. It
took effort to figure out what I was trying to say.
Communicating to form the words was slow and tiresome. I
struggled trying to keep blinking long enough to spell words.
How can this be so hard? I can't even do this simple thing! A
pencil was used to point to each letter. I blinked if it was in that
row. Simple, but it worked. *Trying to express myself is time-con-
suming. This is frustrating! There has to be an easier way.* Just to
say "I love you" took me at least 16 blinks. At this point, I was
so weak that I had about a twenty-blink vocabulary.

During my ICU stay there were heated exchanges between
the doctors and Steven. The doctors offered little hope of my

recovery based on statistics. They wanted Steven to be realistic. I had one chance in a million to live. *I'm treated as if I'm a dead person already. Why are people talking in front of me as if I'm not here? I can hear and understand everything being said.*

Later, I learned from Steven that he felt he had to occupy the position I would recover. If he lost hope of the idea for one moment, one second, I was a dead woman. My chances were one in a million and to realize my chance, someone was going to have to spend a million dollars. The doctors didn't want to, nor the hospital or the insurance company.

It was not just the money; the arithmetic was worse. The doctors told Steven if my life were saved, I would be nothing more than a vegetable. Even though I was a young, strong and healthy woman, I could live fifty years or more hooked up to tubes, unable to talk or move and awake most of the time. I would feel pain but be locked into my body. Steven refused to believe this. His faith, no matter how bleak things got, kept him sane. The staff mistook his constant prayers for a delusional system in which they believed Steven thought he was talking directly to God.

Making matters worse for the staff, within hours of my stroke, the waiting room began filling with fellow church people. At times, there were forty or more people in the waiting room praying for me. They prayed. They sang and brought potluck dinners to the hospital.

Steven was free to be at the hospital because friends were at our house around the clock, day in and day out. Every afternoon and night, a different person would cook for my family.

The waiting room was never empty. Twenty-four hours a day there were people with Steven and people constantly praying for me. A schedule was worked out to guarantee someone that was at the hospital twenty-four hours a day. I was totally and completely helpless. The people watching over me were a great comfort and blessing. Angels surrounded me.

Dr. Jeffrey Saver's Comments:

Patients in the locked-in state are awake and aware but unable to move their limbs or most facial muscles to signal their responsiveness. They do generally retain their ability to blink and to move the eyes up and down. The neural circuitry controlling blinking and vertical gaze resides in the highest portion of the brainstem. This region is usually spared from injuries affecting the rest of the brainstem. As a result, patients can use blinking to communicate. A variety of coding systems have been developed to facilitate communication with the locked-in patient, but even the most sophisticated is frustrating and exhausting to employ. Success requires, as Kate exhibited, a determined and resilient spirit.

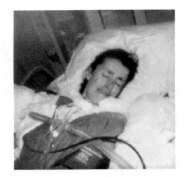

Kate, ICU

CHAPTER FOUR

The Calvary
Comes In All Sizes

etsy, a petite middle-aged woman with auburn hair, was the first therapist to work with me. Every moment she was with me gave me hope. Wearing glasses and a white medical lab coat she used terms I had never heard. To me, Betsy was an example of walking, living hope.

I recall my first meeting with her. Betsy quietly knocked at my door trying not to startle me, coming over to my bedside. Leaning over and gently touching my hand she softly spoke, "Kate, my name is Betsy and I'm from Physical Therapy. How are you this morning? She paused to see if I could comprehend her words. *How am I? I'd be fine if I wasn't here!* Betsy said, "I'll be working with your lower body." *Why do I need you? What's wrong with my body? Why can't I move? I have lots of questions and no way of communicating.* As she leaned over, a tiny gold pin in the shape of an ice skate boot caught my eye. It was attached on the lapel of her jacket. *She must like ice-skating; it's hard to imagine her skating around a rink. If only I could utter my thoughts out loud then maybe I could get some of my questions answered.*

Betsy's voice was soothing and gentle, and I could see she was compassionate about her job. I remember the first time she sat me on the edge of the bed in front of her. Steven and a friend were in my room that morning. A cheerful Betsy came in with her assistant. *Who is he? Is he helping her?* Ron, in his late twenties, was tanned and very muscular. He looked like he could be a lifeguard on the beach, rather than working in a hospital. *I may be sick but you're awfully cute!* I was slightly embarrassed to have him help but I didn't have a choice since I couldn't speak.

I soon learned that Ron was Betsy's hands. The strength she lacked and needed, Ron provided. "We think you might be strong enough to try and sit up on the edge of the bed," she said standing beside Ron. (What they meant was that I would be strong enough to be held up by Ron without passing out.) "Don't worry, Kate, we are here to help you," she said. Betsy wheeled a stool over to the edge of the bed. "Okay, Ron, let's start to sit her up."

My bed was equipped with a special air mattress that helped to prevent bedsores. Ron turned the switch off quickly deflating the mattress. *I feel like I'm sinking and disappearing in this bed!* "Careful, Ron, make sure the lines aren't pulling," Betsy instructed. *Lines aren't pulling! I'm worried about my gown being open!* I was beginning to realize modesty would be a concept without any meaning in this dark twilight world of the sick or dying. Together, working as a team with many maneuvers and attempts, I found myself sitting on the edge of the bed. Ron's strong arms held my frail body. *I feel dizzy. Everything around me is spinning. I don't like this! I want to lie down again. I am not strong enough to sit up. This is so painful.*

"Wow! Look at you, how does that feel?" Betsy said elated. *It feels weird, I prefer being back in bed.* "Pick your head up; keep it up, Kate," she said. *I'm trying! I'm trying! My head feels like a piece of lead. The only thing that feels good is leaning into Ron!* "Hold it up; Kate, don't let your head droop." said Betsy repeating herself. "Do you feel lightheaded or dizzy?" she asked. *I feel like my head is going to drop off and I'm soaked in sweat. This isn't fair. Everything looks fuzzy.* After what felt like an eternity I was sitting up, somewhat with assistance. "How's that, Kate, you're sitting up," Betsy said. "Good job, Kate," Ron said. *I feel weak and sick. Please let me lie down.* "Ron, keep holding onto Kate," she said. My friend Rhonda had reached into her handbag and took out a compact mirror. "Here, Betsy, I have a small mirror for Kate to look at herself," Rhonda said. *Is she crazy? I don't want to look at myself!* Betsy held the mirror up. "There, Kate, you can take a look at yourself." Luckily for me the mirror tilted and all I could see was the ceiling.

Gradually my body started to sway backward. I had no control of my torso. My mouth was closed tight and my head went back into its locked position to the right side. *I need desperately to lie down. I can't sit here anymore. I feel exhausted from the five minutes of sitting here.* Everyone was ecstatic by what they had seen. "Wow, Betsy, that's amazing to see her sitting up like that," Steven said thrilled. I was placed back in bed, feeling relieved to lie down.

The Cavalry kept coming, the PTs, OTs and a Speech Pathologist named Carolyn. She gave me a warm smile when she introduced herself. "Kate, I'm Carolyn from the Speech Pathology Department. How are you today? Can you try to touch the corners of your mouth with your tongue?" she asked. *How am I? Miserable! I want out of here! I'll attempt what you asked.*

"Yes, Kate can do that," Steven said. "Betsy has given us a sheet with simple mouth exercises. I have Kate do those every hour." *Yeah, he doesn't let me forget!* "Good. Okay, Kate, try to imitate me as I do some oral motor commands," Carolyn said. I followed her directions, finding it hard to control my secretions. I blinked yes or no to her simple questions. *I understand everything you are saying. Why can't I speak?*

These exercises are so primitive you could teach them to a monkey. Here I am a grown woman and I can't even move my body. I can't talk, swallow and to help Carolyn is having me stick my tongue out? How can that help me to speak? Yet, Steven kept at me hour after hour. *I hate his nagging but I'm in no shape to fight with anyone.*

Carolyn turned to my husband, "What I'd like to try is attaching a passy-muir valve to her trachea tube. I think Kate is a good candidate for this. It will help her relearn to communicate." *I'd love to be able to speak! I have so much I want to say.* "Wonderful. What is a passy-muir valve?" he asked. "It's a speaking valve that will allow her to control the air in her trachea needed to speak," she said.

Carolyn raised my bed. Leaning over she fit the valve and deflated the cuff. *I'm scared no sounds will come out.* "Okay, Kate, try sounding something," she instructed. *I want to shout! I'm trying to sound out something.* "I-I-," could be heard faintly. Carolyn listened intently. *Why can't I get any words out? I thought this was supposed to help me speak?*

"Try to take it slowly," Carolyn instructed me. Garbled sounds were produced and with the force of me trying to make a sound, the tiny valve catapulted across the room. *Oops! Watch out!* "Look out!" Steven shouted ducking his head. Both of them stood back in amazement. "Well at least we know she has a good set of lungs," Carolyn said laughing. *What happened? I don't understand this!*

"We need to work on this but it will help her a lot," she said. The valve was removed and my cuff on the trachea inflated. "I was told Kate has aphasia," he said. "Aphasia is a total or partial loss of the ability to use words. It appears she understands everything being said to her when I ask simple questions. It will take practice working with the valve," she said. "Are you going to leave the valve with us?" Steven asked. "No, I need to be present when she tries this," Carolyn said putting it in a jar. She then left the room. "Well that was interesting. I can't wait until you can speak again," he said. *Neither can I, this is so frustrating trying to communicate. I only hope my speech comes back.*

"Let's do some leg exercises," he said pulling the sheets back. *I'm tired from trying to speak. Please let me rest.* Steven moved my legs apart. "Okay now try to bring your legs together," he said. I reluctantly did the exercise but refused to try anymore. "Good job, Kate, one more time," he said. *I'm just worn out. I need some rest now.* "Okay you get some rest. I'm going to go out and make sure the nurses chart this," he said. I closed my eyes and dozed off.

While I fought my own battle to stay alive, Steven had a constant battle with the insurance company to keep me from being sent to a long-term care facility. There I would be allowed to spend the rest of life as a water lily. I would get plenty of fresh air getting turned toward the light, but no intense therapy in order for me to walk or talk again. This was a constant reality for Steven. He would have lost the fight if my medical condition were more stable. I just cannot imagine how people without strong advocates can possibly make it through the medical process. Without someone at your side your chances to survive a serious illness are fearfully low.

The best I could do at this point was to sit up with help for thirty minutes each day. The doctor had written orders in my chart to have me sit in a *cardiac chair* three times a day. The following day, Betsy and Ron wheeled this hideous-looking chair into my room. *I'm going to sit in that?* "This is a cardiac chair, Kate, and we'll sit you up for thirty minutes in it," Betsy explained. *A cardiac chair? It looks like something they would put someone in just before electrocuting them. I don't want to sit in that thing!* The chair was brought close to the bed, the back lowered. Now it looked like a gurney. Ron slid my body onto it. I was gently moved as if I was in a coma. *I hope they know what they are doing.* He then raised the back of the chair until I was sitting in an upright position. Betsy started placing pillows behind my neck and back for support. Looking back, I now realize how much I appreciated the expertise in positioning Betsy and Ron used with pillows, towels, and blankets to make me comfortable. It was amazingly painful and exhausting sitting in the chair.

"Let's wheel Kate near the edge of the door so she can watch what's going on," Betsy said. Ron maneuvered the chair, setting the brakes and making sure the lines were reachable from the bed to the chair. "I'll be back soon, Kate," Betsy said as she gave me a final check. *I don't want to be left alone!* With blurred vision, I couldn't make out the people. I saw the fuzzy shapes of nurses scurrying from room to room. I sat there wondering when the thirty minutes would be up. Oprah was on TV but the picture was hazy for me. *This is hopeless, I cannot stand the pain another second. How can I make it thirty minutes? Don't these people know I'm sick? Why can't I speak? I'm trapped in my body! I hate this chair. Oh please, I just want to lie down.*

A nurse reminded me that I had another ten minutes of sitting in the chair. I was so alone—my world was only me. I struggled to communicate with anyone. *My world is beyond my control and beyond my touch. Please help! Someone please help me! I can speak to no one but God. Let someone understand me God. I look like a clone for Dr. Hannibal Lecter. I can do it; I will do it and why complain when there is no one here to offer sympathy.*

I closed my eyes to rest. All I was thinking about were my children. *What would they be feeling now?* I could not remember how long it had been since I had seen them. I knew it was a foolish vanity, and also an instinct to protect them, but I did not want them to see me like this. I still did not know if I would live let alone recover, and I did not want my children to remember me the way I looked in ICU.

Stephanie, my oldest child was so scared. "Where's mom gone?" she would ask. She questioned her daddy several times a day, "Why can't mom pick up the phone and talk to me? Don't they have phones in hospitals? What's she saying? Am I going to see her again? I want to see my mom." Steven kept reassuring her, "She'll be home soon." Yet with each passing day he realized that I was going to be in for the long haul.

I had been in the hospital for a couple of weeks and each day, Steven asked me if Stephanie could come in. *Come in and see me? Are you crazy? I don't want her to see me like this.* I longingly gazed at the picture of Stephanie and Rachel on the shelf. *I wish I could be home with my girls. I miss them so much.* Everyday he would ask, "Can Stephanie come in today?" *No! I don't want my little girl to see me so sick.* I blinked out no on the alphabet board.

He pleaded with me, "Kate, she wants to see you, she thinks you are dead." He had to convince Stephanie that I hadn't died. *Stephanie thinks I am dead. Oh, my poor baby! I love her so much. Perhaps it would be better if I were dead rather than to live like this. God, please help me. I want to live for my children. Give me a miracle!*

Steven felt he had to have Stephanie see me or she would be scarred for life. He came in one day with my friend Cherri and took a few photos of me with a Polaroid camera; I could have killed him for doing it. I remember that morning he took the photos. "Kate, I'm going to take your photo this morning." *Photo! What the heck is he thinking? I may be sick but if I could get up, I'd wring his bloody neck! I don't want photos taken.* "Kate, I have to show Stephanie you are still alive," Steven explained. I struggled to turn my head. *I can't escape this. Oh God, please make him stop.* He took five or six images from different angles. "The girls will be happy to see you haven't died, Kate. Try to smile," Steven said. *Try to smile! I want you to go away!*

Persistently he kept asking. Firmly, I kept blinking out no. *When is he going to quit asking? No! No! No!*

"Kate, you have to let her see you, she loves you," he asked distressed. *Okay, okay, I'll see her!* I reluctantly blinked out yes to him. "Can I bring her today?" he asked enthusiastically. *No! I don't want to see her today.*

He asked a girlfriend of mine to be at the house when he showed the photos to the girls. "I don't want to be alone, Valerie," he said anxiously. "No problem, I'll help you," she said. He prepared the girls for what they were about to see. "Sit down next to daddy, girls. I'm going to let you see a photograph of mom. She's very sick but slowly getting better." He pulled one of the prints from his wallet. "This is what your mother looks like in the hospital," he said handing it to them.

Stephanie held the snapshot and paused for a long time while she studied it. "What is that daddy?" she asked pointing. "Oh that's a tube to help mom breathe and that funny thing on her arm takes her blood pressure," he said. "That helps the doctors and nurses make your mother get better," Valerie said. "How can that help?" she asked puzzled. "It tells them what is going on inside her body," she explained. "Oh," Stephanie said gazing at the photo, teardrops starting to run down her cheeks. This doesn't look like mom," she said. Choking back his tears he said, "I know honey, she's very ill."

Stephanie ran out of the room with the photo. "My mom doesn't look like this," she said screaming. Rachel sat with her dad and refused to look at the photograph. She was already referring to the nanny at the time as her mom. He turned to Valerie, "This was a mistake. It's too soon to have shown them this." Stephanie had hidden the photo. "That's not my mother. I know she wants to see me. Let me visit her, daddy," she pleaded tugging at his shirt. She didn't believe I was that ill. "I want to see mom if she's alive," she cried. He sat her on his lap. "I know, honey, you will," he said gently rocking her in his arms. "We need to pray that mom keeps getting better."

One afternoon while in my room, he inquired again about Stephanie coming in to see me. *This guy just doesn't let up! He's so persistent. Fine! I don't care anymore.* For whatever the reason, I blinked "yes" to him. Overjoyed, he hurried out of the room to call the nanny. "Amanda, bring Stephanie down. Kate's ready to see her," he instructed. "Hurry before she changes her mind," he hastily said.

I was lying in bed doing leg exercises with my therapist Betsy when Rhonda emerged at the door knocking gently, "Stephanie is here, Kate." *She's here already? I'm working with Betsy. Now isn't a good time.* All of a sudden my husband came into view holding Stephanie. Betsy pulled the sheets up on the bed. "Hi Stephanie, come on in and see mom. We were doing some exercises on her legs." Stephanie clung to her dad, her arms tight around his neck. "Go over and see mom," he said, putting her down.

Stephanie, it's Mum! I wish I could reach out and touch you. Don't be scared honey. I miss you so much; I just want to hold you. She stood there gazing at me. The surroundings frightened her. I lay there looking at her, yearning to touch her. *I wonder what you are thinking? If only I could hold your hand. You look frightened.* Stephanie didn't quite know how to react; she hesitated taking a step forward. *That's it, honey come over to mom.*

Afraid, she ran back to her father, "Daddy, daddy." He bent down scooping her up in his arms. "It's okay, honey, that's your mom, remember the photo I showed you?" he said. She didn't respond and turned her head away from me. She started crying, letting out the most awful wail. I shall never forget the sound of her anguished cry. Steven said he could have sworn that both Stephanie and I were screaming in unison. "Take me home daddy," she said in between her sobbing. *I wish you had not brought her in. This has been too painful for both of us!*

Betsy tried to encourage everyone by making light conversation, "Stephanie, mom's getting better, she'll be home soon," she said. The tension in the air was thick; you could cut it with a knife. I lay there with my eyes watering. *I just want to hold my little girl.* It was traumatic for both of us. Betsy even fought back the tears in her eyes. "I think I had better take her home," Steven said. "I'll be back later tonight Kate."

After they left, Betsy positioned me in the bed. She rolled some towels and placed them at my feet to prevent the foot drop. "Oh, Kate, your daughter is darling," she said. *Yes. I wish I could be with her. I miss them both.* Betsy left the room so I could rest. *This is the hardest time in my life. Why, God, why do I have to endure this?*

Ten tips that psychologist, Judith Carl, Ph.D. has found to help children through the process of Mom and Dad having any type of adversity.

1. Expect that your children (of all ages) will have feelings, thoughts and opinions about whatever the issue/problem is.

2. Even though you may not talk about the problem in earshot of your children, they will pick up the 'vibes' that there is something wrong.

3. It helps to calm children, to let them know that there is a problem. What you tell them of the details depends on the issue, crisis, or problem.

4. Certain crisis need to be talked about in as much detail as children want, i.e., accidents, terrorism, life-threatening events (hospitalizations). They need to be reassured that the other parent will be there to talk about it as they have a need to. Some children need to hear and be told that it is not their fault.

5. If it is a life situation; i.e. possible divorce, separation, etc., children need to know there is a problem, that they did not cause it, and that they are loved by both parents. However, they do NOT need to hear and know the details of the problem.

6. Keep children out of the "middle" of the problem. For example, do not have them be the messenger between the parents, or ask them to choose which parent they want to live with, or ask how they feel about what Mom or Dad did or said.

7. Acknowledge your children's feelings. Examples: "I can see you're upset about this . . . You must really be worried about . . . I am here and available to talk to you whenever you have a question or just want to talk. Let me know."

8. It is okay to let them see your emotions, feelings. And, in fact, much of the time it helps them to see that you have feelings too. Feelings are different from details. Feelings are sadness, hurt, fear, relief, joy, calmness, anticipation, etc. that surround the details of the situation. It lets them know that it is okay for them to have their own feelings.

9. Consider some outside counseling or therapy for your children if it seems that they are having difficulties because of the situation or crisis. You may see it in their school grades, detachment if normally outgoing, isolation, a sudden change in their behavior at home or school; i.e. acting out, extreme introversion, stop eating, or binge eating, problems with friends, etc.

10. Asking for help for yourself and or family is a strength and courageous. You and your family, including your children, deserve to have the support, guidance, and help in getting through any crisis or life situation.

CHAPTER FIVE

The Light

The only family I had nearby was my husband and the girls. My biological family was in New Zealand. Steven called them the first night I was in the hospital leaving a message on their voice-mail to call him as soon as possible. Briefly he explained I was in the hospital with a suspected stroke. Mum's first reaction was, "There's no way, Kate's too fit and healthy. He has to be exaggerating." She phoned my father at work, and he too, was stunned, as were my siblings. My brother Tony, a pharmacist, thought it was probably a severe migraine, "She's too fit to have had a stroke." Steven kept my parents informed and after numerous calls to the States and New Zealand, my parents realized how grave things were.

The church was my extended family, giving a tremendous amount of support. As the news spread quickly throughout the church, people began praying, cooking, visiting, babysitting, and helping in numerous ways. They cared for the girls, cleaned my house, did my laundry, walked my dog, grocery shopped and cooked the meals. Some were recruited to spend time with the children. Other women sat with me twenty-four hours a day and still others prepared meals for my family. These people only wanted to help and didn't want anything in return.

The waiting room in ICU was constantly full of people day after day. A member donated a journal for people to sign and express their prayers and wishes for me.

Women from the church sat quietly by my bedside reading the bible and praying. It was a one-way conversation as I lay there listening. *I wonder if they know I can understand what's being said?* Nurses came in and out continuing with their daily duties. *Why God. Why me? Why am I hooked up to machines and totally helpless here?* Women constantly massaged lotion on my feet, and others filed my nails to keep them short. Rolled up wash cloths were placed in each palm to help tone my hands. (Today I keep my nails trimmed to prevent them from digging into my palm. I have learned to control the tone in my left hand. As I wake up in the morning now, my hand is clenched tight in a fist. Gently I open each finger. Acrylic nails are definitely out of the question!)

Often a couple of friends would wash my hair. My hair was long requiring a whole can of dry shampoo. *This is agonizing to have my hair washed and it feels like an eternity lying here.* After the shampoo process, my hair was braided. *I feel relieved that's over! It's nice my friends are taking care of the little details. Am I ever going to make it out of here? Please, God let me have my life back.*

I recall one evening when my friends Susan and Lisa were in my room visiting. *It feels good having my feet massaged except for this annoying strand of hair by my eye. There's no way I can remove that yet how can I communicate to them how annoying this is?* I lay there frustrated. *I just want to scratch the heck out of my face!* Both women noticed I was trying to communicate something.

"Do you need a nurse?" Susan asked. *No I need this hair off my face!* "Are you comfortable?" Lisa asked. *If only I could express what I need to you both.* "I wonder what she's trying to tell us?" Susan said, a puzzled look on her face. *I feel like we are playing Jeopardy! This is a simple task to remove a hair that's bothering me yet it's so hard for me to communicate this! I've taken so much for granted in life.*

The women tried to guess what I needed. *It's no use! I'll never be able to tell you! Is this how my life is going to be?* 49

After a lengthy amount of time they finally guessed what was bothering me. "I know," Lisa said excitedly. "It's a hair that's bugging you," she said running her hand across my face. *Yes! Finally you guessed! That feels better already!* "Kate, I'm sorry that took us so long to figure that out," Susan said. *I can't believe how frustrating that was!*

I was desperately sick for the seventy days I was in ICU, and listed critical for sixty-nine of those days. I had lived through the trauma of an insult to my brain, but at a dreadful price. Weighing only ninety-eight pounds, all the doctors knew was that I would be faced with serious medical complications. The first complication was mild, a blood clot in my leg. The doctor caught it early before it could lead to another stroke. Technically I had phlebitis in my leg, but in my condition if the clot had traveled to my lungs, I would have died.

When I first regained motion, Steven saw me move one of my fingers. It took him two days to get anyone to believe him. Suddenly here was this man telling the doctors that this totally paralyzed woman had moved her fingers. The doctors thought he was nuts and politely told him that family members often see what they want. Steven would not relent. He kept working with me and insisted the doctor come to see for himself. I almost lost my chance to receive therapy at this point, because I had exhausted myself from attempting this simple task, so that when the doctor did come, I could not move anything. I lost all power to move from sheer exhaustion. Steven knew the doctor would not come back in to see me move. He went to convince the nurses. Finally I was able to slightly move for a nurse and she noted it in the chart for the doctor to see. The doctor felt duty bound to check out the chart notes and when he was in my room, he thought he saw me move, or did he? He simply refused to believe his own eyes. The doctor insisted on coming back two more times before he believed I had voluntarily moved any part of my body. After the third time he told Steven that he wasn't easily impressed, but this impressed him. This was something extraordinary and he thought there was a possibility that I could achieve a significant recovery.

Officially, I was still on the track to be put into a skilled nursing facility to simply gather up sunshine. No one believed I had any real potential for recovery except Steven and the church. They believed I would be granted a miracle. The odds of making any significant recovery were less than one chance in a million.

Making things worse, Steven told the doctors that while praying at my bedside, he had seen the room turn bright as the sun, feeling the presence of God. From that point on, he told everyone I would have a miracle. I know he believes he saw the light and believed I would get better. Steven was right I think on both counts. The power of prayer is amazing!

Steven kept close contact with my parents, and at the request of doctors, called them to learn my family history. He told them that I had either a stroke or a brain tumor. "Strokes did not run in my family," Mum said. "However Kate had an uncle who died of a brain tumor at the age of 46." Mum had to call my aunt to get more details. My aunt phoned Steven back with the information. Mum waited anxiously for further news. When Steven did call my parents with the new information that it was a stroke, both clung to each other weeping with relief. They, of course, had no idea how serious a stroke could be, but it seemed much less serious than a brain tumor.

I had survived the stroke and now suddenly the doctors found that I was growing a bacterium called *pseudomonas* in my trachea tube. That would not have been so frightening except the tested culture showed that it was not responsive to any known antibiotic. This was a super bug that only grew in hospitals and if it spread from my breathing tubes into my lungs I would die. The doctors felt helpless since they could not find any antibiotic to treat this bug. We were fortunate that the man running the lab at the hospital was a member of our church. Usual protocol for a culture was every two days, but Dr. Kolodney and the lab conspired to do a culture for me every two hours.

This was one of Steven's lowest moments. He waited for each successive culture to come back from the lab. Results were showing that the bacterium was growing faster and faster, it seemed inevitable that having lived through the stroke, I would die of a bacterial infection.

The doctors told Steven I had two or three days at the most to live unless a solution could be found. Steven started to hound the doctors working my case. "What if we do this, what if we do that, can we try this?" Steven questioned Dr. Kolodney. He did not let up. Dr. Kolodney spent a whole hour talking with Steven, and they finally decided to call an infectious disease specialist. He came, took one look at me and explained to Steven and the doctor that he might have some magic. He sprayed what seemed like Lysol into the tube, and the bacterium was killed. The doctors were trying to treat me by giving antibiotics through my IVs. The medicine could not reach the point where it would have been a strong enough dose to kill the infection in the trachea tube. By spraying it directly on the site of the infection, a large enough dose could be delivered to kill the bacteria. Steven sat hour after hour as the bacteria count continued to go down, down and then out. I had now survived my third medical crisis.

My fourth crisis was not life threatening but certainly one of the most hellish things that I had to endure. Since I could not receive nourishment through an IV tube, a G-tube had been placed in my stomach. Through the tube I received foods like Ensure and other supplements. Perhaps because of the antibiotic or just because of my immobility I was now unable to have a bowel movement. Ensure through a tube is far from tasty but it does keep you free from feeling hungry. I was so constipated that the doctors were forced to turn off the feeding tube. Then the count started: Day one: no food and no bowel movement. Day two: the same results were produced. Day three: still neither food nor a bowel movement. I was now seventy-two hours without food.

I was starving. I thought I was going insane. I was screaming out in my mind, *Don't you know I need to eat!* The hunger pangs were unbearable. This continued for another five days. I could think of nothing but eating and having a damn bowel movement! The pressure on my stomach was awful. Up to this point the bagful of Ensure passing through the tube, sounded pretty good. *I just want something!*

Day eight: still nothing happened. Finally on Day nine, I had a bowel movement and the doctors were able to gradually start me back on Ensure. The agony of going without food was a constant pain that lasted not several hours like the surgery to put the tube in, but several days. My whole body cried out, *Feed me. I'm alive and a person in here, don't let me die. For God's sake, somebody feed me!*

It would take another week to get me up to a dose that would allow me to be free from hunger pangs.

After that ordeal, I was hauled out of my room and put on a sling like a cow or pig and moved onto a scale. This continued once a week, very early in the mornings. *What is happening?* I felt the cold air as the sheets were gathered back. *Please let me sleep. I want my covers back!* In a dreamlike state, I remember being moved around while I kept my eyelids closed. Discreetly I was rolled onto my side, while one nurse slipped a heavy piece of canvas under me. They repeated the process on my other side. I heard the clicking of metal and the cranking of a handle. *What are they doing?* Without warning, I felt myself gradually lifting and being suspended in the air. My eyelids quickly opened. *What's happening?*

"Just relax, Kate, we are weighing you," said one of the nurses. *Weighing me?* The noise of the cranking stopped and I remained there while the nurses wrote in my chart. I feel tremendous empathy now when I see a helpless animal being lifted in the air from a dangerous situation. Suspended in the air, one is powerless. That's how I felt! What seemed like an eternity actually took only a few minutes. *Isn't there a more dignified way of weighing someone?* The nurses would lower the device and put me back in bed and pull up the sheets. *How am I supposed to go back to sleep?*

The machine for weighing patients was called a sling scale. (Since my stroke, the hospital has acquired a device that's attached to the bed which weighs the patient.) My weight over the six weeks in ICU went down considerably. My once-toned body faded to a mere ninety pounds. I had nowhere to go, but up.

Steven continuously phoned my parents, begging them to come, yet they could not afford the trip. My church offered to pay for my parent's round trip tickets, but Mum and Dad were too proud to accept the help. Both appreciated the gesture but felt a trip later on would be more helpful. Dad was self-employed, and could not leave his business.

While at the hospital one morning Steven approached the charge nurse. "Could you do me a favor?" he asked. "My mother-in-law does not realize how sick Kate is. She thinks I'm exaggerating. If I call her will you talk to her?" Steven asked. "Sure, I'll talk with her," the nurse said. He dialed the number. A brief conversation took place. "My daughter isn't going to die is she?" Mum asked. The nurse replied, "I can't tell you that your daughter is not going to die. She is in critical condition. Mrs. Adamson, Kate is very sick and I know if she was my daughter I'd want to be here for her." There was a brief silence and Mum answered, "I'll make plans to come straight away. Thank you nurse."

The New Zealand Airline plane landed in Los Angeles on a Sunday. Mum was anxious to see me but had to go through the long customs line before finally seeing Steven. The two had only met twice in person. Mum explained to him, "I would like to go straight to the hospital to see Kate." In the car Steven showed her a couple of photos he had taken of me in ICU. "Surely she doesn't look like this?" she said. "I'm afraid so," Steven replied. Mum sat in the back saying nothing. Despite the 15-hour flight and her exhaustion, she was overwhelmed with mixed emotions.

Mum was determined to see me that afternoon. Steven noticed that she appeared to have caught a cold. He suggested she wear a surgical mask and gloves when she came near me.

Steven and Mum arrived at Torrance Memorial Hospital mid- afternoon. It was a beautiful day for the outside world, but Mum paid no attention to the surroundings. All she wanted to do was see her daughter. They made their way to ICU. My friend Penny came into my room. "Your mom is here; just enjoy her and let her love you, Kate," she said. *Mum is here?* Moments later when I saw her standing in the doorway, her face looked gaunt from worry, she paused for a moment glancing around the room at the faces of four women standing by my bed. A couple of the women were rubbing lotion on my hands and feet. I looked at Mum and opened my mouth to cry out, but no sound came. *Mum, mum, you are here. Thank God you have come!*

Seeing Mum standing at the foot of my bed, I knew I must be very sick for her to have come that far. It suddenly dawned on me that I might actually die. *Where's dad? Why isn't he here?* She stood where I could see the tears filling her eyes. *Mum, I wish I could speak to you; I have so much to tell you.* Jenny, another friend, was massaging my arms, "See Katie, your Mom did come."

"Do you have a cold?" Jenny asked my mother. "A slight one. I just left winter in New Zealand," Mum replied in her thick accent. "We need you to put a mask on if you want to come close," Jenny explained. "I'm her mother and nothing I do could possibly hurt her," she replied. Teardrops trickled down her cheeks as she approached my bed. Pulling a handkerchief from her pocket she wiped her tears. She leaned over gently kissing me on the forehead. "Why Katie, why?" Mum asked weeping. *Mum, I wish I knew the answer.*

Mum leaned over again to kiss me. Jenny quickly spoke, "Oh, you can't go too near her." Straightening up, and turning to Jenny, Mum said, "Excuse me, she's my daughter." She leaned over and kissed me on the forehead. "You remind me of that little girl when you used to get sick," she said stroking my forehead and smiling. I silently wept to myself. *Mum, why has this happened?*

In order to hide her emotions, she prattled on about her plans to be here for five weeks. Mum chitchatted about everyone else in New Zealand and told me there would be a surprise when she had to leave. *I wonder what that is? Must be a family member coming over. I don't care about a surprise. I just want to go home.* I previously had plans with my brother Tony to visit Disneyland in August but not anymore. My sister and brother were planning to come in August to spend some time with me. *I really don't want them to see me like this.* "Your father couldn't come. He had to stay home and do the business. He sends his love and I'm to call him every day to keep him informed," she said. "Everyone, everyone sends his or her love," she stressed. As she was catching me up on all the gossip, I realized that the day of my stroke was her birthday. *I can't believe my stroke was on her birthday! This is one birthday she won't forget.*

A nurse came in asking everyone to leave while she attended to my needs. Mum left with the ladies and sat outside. She had brought some photos of my siblings and me. Like a proud mother she showed everyone her family. As everyone came back into the room, Steven explained that he was driving Mum home so she could get some rest and see the girls. "I'm very tired Katie babes; it was a long flight," Mum said. *I wish I could go with you, don't leave me.* She kissed me on the cheek and left the room.

The pain and loneliness was so overwhelming that I could hardly tell what was reality and what was a dream. Hours had no meaning. Days had no meaning. It was all one endless eternal dark and painful exile in hell.

CHAPTER SIX

Rehabilitation:
The Next Step

t was a comfort knowing Mum was here. I knew she would keep things in order around the house. Mum enjoyed meeting Betsy and watching her therapy routine. The nurses enjoyed hearing Mum's New Zealand accent. A frequent question Mum encountered was, "Does your daughter sound like you?"

On Monday morning while watching my therapy session, Mum asked Betsy if it would be possible to hold me in her arms. *Oh Mum, not now! They are too busy for that. Besides I don't want to be embarrassed!* "I just want to hold my daughter," she said politely. Her voice sounded muffled through the mask that she finally gave into wearing. "Oh sure," Betsy said. *Oh my God, don't you people realize how much effort that's going to take?* Carefully Ron and Betsy sat me on the edge of the bed, being cautious not to pull any lines. "Oh, thank you Betsy and Ron," Mum said coming over to me. She wrapped her arms tight around me; my frail body felt her warmth. *Mum, I can smell your perfume as you are holding me. I love you. I know this is hard on you too. I'm thirty-three years old, but not at this moment; I'm just a child in your arms.*

As she gently held me, I could hear her quietly weeping. *What's going to happen to me Mum?* "Oh, Katie, I love you darling. It breaks my heart to see you like this," Mum said whispering. She glanced up at Betsy. "Kate's awfully thin. Isn't there something the doctor can do?" There was nothing left of me but bare skin and bones. "Yes, you could speak to Dr. Kolodney about building her up more," said Betsy. *Mum! You have always felt I was too thin!* The very next day I was increased to 1,000 calories a day through my feeding tube. I knew Mum had spoken to the doctor.

Mum watched Betsy stretching the heel cord on my foot, and the procedure made her curious. "What does that do, Betsy?" she asked. The stretch felt good. Betsy paused for a moment. "This is to prevent her foot from developing foot drop. In fact Mrs. Adamson, it would be beneficial if Kate wore some high-top tennis shoes a few hours everyday." *Tennis shoes? Tennis shoes in bed! No way! I'm in a hospital sick!* Mum was only too willing to help, "What size do I get?" Betsy replied, "You will want a couple of sizes bigger than she normally wears. Right now her feet are swollen."

The problem was to have the tennis shoes fit tightly enough, but not so tight that they hurt. June (Mum) and a friend, Deborah Ward, made several trips to the local stores trying to find the right pair. It was a guessing game to see if they would fit and not hurt. *I can't tell if these are okay. I don't want to wear shoes in bed! These are hideous looking!* Mum finally found a pair that Betsy felt was appropriate. I wore the shoes for four hours a day keeping my feet in an upright position. The tops were cut off some socks and placed on my feet, which were constantly cold from poor circulation.

It was enjoyable having Mum visit each day. She delicately smoothed lotion on my face. My arms were dry and scaly from the blood pressure cuff being left on, so she smoothed lotion on my arms. She knew to scratch my dry skin, and it felt wonderful. She combed and braided my hair. *Someone should probably cut my hair, but I've lost too much to lose anything more.* Mum chatted about everyone back home trying to take my mind off my stroke. "I've bought you some of your favorite licorice, Kate," she said eagerly. *I can't wait to have some. Maybe I can eat some in rehab.* "I filled an empty shoe box, Kate, so you will have plenty," she said laughing. *A shoe box full? I'd love some now, Mum.*

I was thirsty all the time. I had no swallowing reflexes. I had to settle for mouth swabs or occasionally Mum would sneak me an ice chip. *A big bottle of orange Gatorade would be great. I can taste it.* I dreamed about Gatorade. I don't know why, I've never been a fan of it. Mum constantly rolled the swabs around my lips and inside my mouth. The lemon tasting swabs didn't quench my thirst. *If only I could swallow some liquid.* My lips were parched and cracked; Mum kept Chap-Stick on those. At mid-morning she briefly left to grab a bite to eat in the cafeteria. *Thank goodness no one eats around me. The smell of food would drive me insane!*

Steven began the long, hard process of getting me accepted into a rehab program. (I'm horrified to tell you that today the program I was in has been closed, and, therefore, it is even harder than it was in 1995 to get help. In 1985, the average hospital stay for a stroke like mine would have been about nine months.) To recover I would need physical therapy and lots of it. The cost would be astronomical. Daniel Freeman was asking $18,000 a week for just the bed, on top of that would be added medication and doctors' fees.

A lady showed up unannounced at my hospital bed, asking Steven all kinds of questions. She had a clipboard and wrote comments as he spoke. I did not realize at the time that my whole future rested with this woman and her report; my fate would be sealed. I remember this incident as if it were yesterday. She seemed pleasant and talked about being admitted into their program and what they offered. *What the heck is she talking about? I don't even know this woman.*

Steven made dozens of calls determining that Daniel Freeman had the best program in Los Angeles and the whole country. He opted for me to be transferred to Daniel Freeman. He was told I would be accepted, but unbeknownst to him, there was no intention on the part of the hospital to accept me. Steven was told I would be transferred to Daniel Freeman Hospital only if I could spend two days on a regular floor to show I was stable enough to be moved. My future, if the insurance companies and the hospital had its way, was a one-way ticket to vegetable-land.

Mum had been in the United States for a couple of weeks when I was finally moved out of ICU onto another floor. *I'm finally leaving ICU. I'm nervous. I don't want to move. I've gotten used to the nurses in ICU.* Steven insisted I be put into a private room away from any sick patients. The doctor wanted to transfer me to a medical floor, but Steven wanted me to go to a surgical floor where there would be less chance of contracting an infection. Dr. Kolodney, amazed that Steven had thought the problem out in such depth, immediately agreed. In ICU each patient shared one nurse. On the surgical floor one nurse was supposed to handle seven patients, but the reality was one nurse for twelve patients.

Mum followed alongside the bed as an attendant wheeled me down the hallway. "This is a good sign, Katie babes. It means you are getting better," she said. *I just want to go home Mum. I wish I could walk out of here.* I was taken to the sixth floor where I stayed for a couple of days. The room was small and Mum put the photos of my daughters where I could see them. I was not quite ready for a regular room; I still had too many secretions. Compared to ICU, the surgical room was paradise.

Mum was given the opportunity to stay the night in the bed next to me. *There's no way she'll do that. The noise of the machines will drive her crazy.* I was surprised to hear she was coming. *Wow! She is going to sleep overnight?* She came that afternoon with her small overnight bag. It was reassuring to know she was there. She made herself comfortable and I drifted off to sleep with her sitting up against the wall reading her book. She had the bathroom door slightly open letting enough light in for her to see. Occasionally, I'd open my eyes to check and see if she was still there. Mum probably got very little sleep that night but I felt safe having her there. Steven was able to get a good-night's sleep; he had been spending fifteen hours a day with me. Besides that he had to father our 18-month-old and 3-year-old daughters.

On his early morning rounds, Dr. Kolodney saw Mum sleeping by me. "Good morning June, you stayed with your daughter last night?" he said. "Good morning doctor. Yes I slept in the spare bed. I'm a little concerned with Kate being on sleeping medication. Can we get her off that doctor?" Mum asked, concerned. *Mum! Are you crazy? I need this. You don't have to lie here with a tube out of your throat.* "Mrs. Adamson, right now is not the appropriate time to take a patient off sleeping medication. I can assure you she won't get addicted," Dr. Kolodney told her.

Dr. Kolodney asked Mum to step outside for a moment. *Damn! I can't hear what he's saying.* I listened intensely, I barely made out what he was saying but I heard the word "limp." *Limp? I'm going to have a limp?* In the hallway he put his arms on hers, "Your daughter will be fine, she'll probably have a limp but she'll be able to live with that." Mum was relieved, "Thank you doctor for everything you've done." I was excited to think this doctor believed in my chances for recovery.

I spent three drawn-out days in anticipation of being transferred to rehab. *When can I go to rehab? I can't go on much longer. I need some hope.*

Dr. Kolodney came by on his daily rounds. "Hi Kate. How are you this morning?" he asked. I slowly blinked my eyes. *How am I? I want out of here.* I blinked out, *Am I going to die?* "I think she's trying to ask you something," Steven said, grabbing the alphabet board and asking me to blink as he pointed to each letter. Dr. Kolodney stood by watching in amazement. "A . . ." Steven said going along each row, writing the letter down. "M . . . I . . . " he said. Then starting at the beginning he went through each row again. "G . . . Am I going to die?" he quickly sounded out.

Yes, that's what I'm trying to ask you. Am I going to die Dr. Kolodney? I waited patiently for the doctor's response. Dr. Kolodney held my hand, "No, you are not going to die. We are getting you transferred to a rehab hospital and getting you back on your feet." *That is reassuring to hear you say that. I feel as if I'm going to give up if I don't get into some therapy. I can't do this any more.*

"Just don't give up, Kate, you have come this far. We will get you into rehabilitation as soon as possible and you'll come home walking," Steven said. *I hope so.* "Hang in there, Kate, we are getting you transferred," Dr. Kolodney said. They walked down the hallway. "We need to get her transferred or I think she will give up her will to live," Dr. Kolodney said. "Yes, I saw a light in Kate's eyes when you told her she wasn't going to die," Steven said. "I've been a doctor for many years and I've never seen anyone go through this much agony."

There was some confusion as to whether I was going to Daniel Freeman Hospital. The doctor kept waiting on an ambulance. On the third day Steven paged Dr. Kolodney to find out why it hadn't arrived. "The ambulance will be there at 10 a.m. tomorrow. There was a problem with the paper work. Don't worry. We'll get her transferred," he said. *Why am I still here? I thought I was being transferred to another hospital.*

Bright and early the next day Mum was ready with some things that I would need in my new hospital room. The lobby was full of friends waiting to wave goodbye to me. The morning came and went with no sign of an ambulance to transfer me. *What could have gone wrong? Don't they know how sick I am? How can they make me wait like this?* No ambulance came that day and suddenly I was racked with fear. I was sure a mistake had happened and that I would be picked up tomorrow at 10 a.m. Dr. Kolodney asked Steven to step out of the room to have a talk. They both walked back to the doctor's office.

Dr. Kolodney retrieved my file on the computer screen which noted that I had been denied admission to Daniel Freeman. "I don't understand what's going on," he said. "Why would the hospital deny her?" Steven asked. "I don't know, but if she hasn't been transferred by noon tomorrow, let's meet in the staff lounge and find out what's going on," Dr. Kolodney said. Steven, with a confused look on his face, spoke, "I don't understand how an ambulance could be delayed two days in a row. Maybe this was intentional?" "Well, we'll get to the bottom of this," Dr. Kolodney said.

The next morning everyone was anxiously waiting for the ambulance to come. *Something is wrong. I'm not going to be transferred. The ambulance isn't going to come, is it? Why do these things have to happen to me? Why can't this be a smooth transition?*

"I'll be back in a moment, Kate, I need to go and call Dr. Kolodney. I'm going to find out why the ambulance hasn't arrived," Steven said. He paged the doctor and sat waiting in the lounge. "The ambulance hasn't arrived and we have to get this done today. In my best medical judgment your wife will die tonight. She will give up her will to live. I am going to call over there," Dr. Kolodney said when he arrived. He dialed the number reaching the admission office and handed the phone to Steven.

As he was speaking to the admissions woman he quickly became irate. "Here, you see if you can get a straight answer," Steven said handing the phone to the doctor. The doctor remained calm as he was speaking and then finally became annoyed. "This woman needs to be transferred, please send an ambulance now," he pleaded. Steven got on the phone and started yelling, "Look I understand what is going on here. You are afraid I will sue you because I'm a lawyer. I have no intention of suing anyone unless your ambulance does not come over here. If there is no ambulance here in two hours then I will sue you and I will see to it that I take depositions of everyone who has ever worked at your hospital." This was a complete bluff on Steven's part, but luckily the admissions department did not include any attorneys. Steven went on to say, "Look, you can be afraid of being sued and that will get you sued for sure or you can take a chance and treat a sick woman just like the Hippocratic oath requires, and you may not get sued. The choice is yours." Steven then handed the phone back to the doctor who again screamed his lungs out. It was finally decided an ambulance would be sent for me that day.

I remember that Friday morning when I was transferred. Mum, Steven and a couple of friends were in my room. Two ambulance attendants came in with a gurney. *Thank you God! My prayer was answered.* The men carefully transferred me onto it and wheeled me downstairs cautiously while Steven held my hand. Gently I was put into the ambulance. I found out later they were the same men who had taken me to the hospital at the onset of my stroke. "You'll be okay, Katie babes, I'm following right behind," Mum said. *Mum! Please don't leave me. I'm scared.* "Don't worry, Kate, I'll be sitting with you in the back and my name is Darryl," said the attendant. *Oh God, please transport me safely. I don't know what's going to happen but give me the strength to do the therapy.*

Later while in rehab these two men visited me and they told me they were just as scared about transferring me as I was. I had to be moved while I was still hooked up to IVs. A stomach tube and an oxygen tank were attached to me. I was as frail as anyone they could remember transporting. They were very frightened I was going to go Code Blue in the ambulance and that they might even lose me during transportation. I looked far more dead than alive that summer afternoon as our meager little band of human beings made its slow progression toward the new hospital. I was in the ambulance, Steven's car followed and a friend's car followed behind him. The whole thing was eerie, like a funeral procession.

The ride to the hospital seemed to take forever. I lay there, watching through windows. *I can see trees. I wonder what area this is?* Darryl constantly checked my vital signs and kept an oxygen mask on me. *I feel like I can't breathe.* "Take deep slow breaths, Kate, we are almost there," he said. We arrived at Daniel Freeman and Mum stayed with me. Steven went to the admissions office. *How long will I be here?* "This looks like a nice hospital, Kate," Mum said. *I don't want to be here. I'd rather be at home. What's going to happen to me?*

There I was lying on a gurney in the lobby of the hospital and it did not seem as if anyone knew I was coming or what to do with me. Steven did his best to solve the problem. There was no paper work on my case that anyone could find. I waited and waited. *What if I get sent back to Torrance Memorial Hospital?* It took about an hour and half before we left for the two-north east wing set aside for spinal and brain injuries. The private room was small and plain with a crucifix of Jesus on the wall.

I was going to be spending three months at this hospital. Mum taped pictures the girls had drawn and some Bible verses on the wall. One of those verses was Isaiah 40:31; "But they that wait upon the Lord shall renew their strength; they shall mount up with wings as eagles; they shall run, and not be weary; and they shall walk, and not faint." I held onto the faith that I would walk again. Another verse was Philippians 4:13, "You can do all things through Christ who strengthens you." I never gave up hope that I would walk again. I had come this far. *Surely God would not abandon me now?*

That afternoon I met the team I would be working with. Because of the extent of brain damage I had suffered I was placed on the spinal cord team. This was a team of people who primarily worked with only spinal cord injuries, quads and hemiplegics. These patients did not usually walk again. I met my new neurologist who would be overseeing me while staying in rehab, Dr. Alexander. I remember being very scared. *I don't want to meet a new team of people. I just want to go home.* I met different people who briefly popped into my room. They included an occupational therapist, physical therapist, head nurse, dietician and others.

The final person was Dr. Alexander and he asked my family to step outside while he did a quick assessment of me. I lay there while he looked at me. *I wonder what he is thinking? Am I going to get better?* He then said, "Yes, I think this will work. We will first need to get rid of the catheter, then the trachea tube and finally the feeding tube. I think you will do well in rehab." I needed to hear those words of encouragement. That afternoon I had met the fifteen-person team of people who would be working with me. *I can't believe how many people are going to be working with me. I just want to get better and get out of here. I have met no one who has told me I'll get better. Isn't there someone I can speak to who has gone through this?*

Steven had a talk with Dr. Alexander and found out that the hospital had not wanted to take me because the evaluation had been so negative. They had seen me before I had miraculously regained my movement. The woman who saw me that day in ICU, saw a woman frozen into a fetal position rigid and showing no signs of life. The woman she saw looked brain dead.

Her report to the hospital had been that I had no potential for rehabilitation. No one bothered to inform the Daniel Freeman staff that I had made tremendous progress. The staff was amazed when they saw me and how responsive I now was. Everyone got excited. I had found a place where I was going to get the best treatment possible. My team was dedicated and I had the support of my family.

CHAPTER SEVEN

No Time for Tears

recall my first self-care session with Joyce. It was Monday morning and she poked her head in through the side of my curtain. "I'll be back in five minutes," she said. What's going to happen next? She returned with a bowl of warm water, a towel, wash cloth and a bar of soap. *Not the sponge bath*! I started crying as she approached me. *My life has been turned upside down.* I started sobbing uncontrollably. *I have gone through six weeks of feeling like a piece of meat; being passed from one nurse to another and now it's beginning again. I can't give up now.*

Joyce placed the items on the side table, wheeling it beside me. In a stern voice she said, "We have no time for tears, Kate. We have work to do." *This woman should show some compassion. Look what I've been through!* "I know you are frightened but crying isn't going to help. Save the tears for later Kate," she said. *I can see I can't cry around you.* I decided from this point on that when Joyce approached me, I would hold back the tears no matter how hard I had to try. *I know she is right; crying is not going to get me to walk again or get me home to the girls. I need to stay strong. I can do this!*

Joyce elevated the bed gently leaning me forward to remove my hospital gown. The cold air made a chill run down my spine. *You're not the one lying here. It's freezing!* She lay me back down and nestled the washcloth in my hand. Joyce put her hand over mine and started gently caressing my skin. "That's it, Kate, follow along with me," she said. It was a slow process and I was freezing, as I lay there naked. I started crying again. *How is this going to help? This is depressing to be in this position. I used to be able to bathe myself and now I can do nothing.*

We finished with the sponge bath and Joyce dried me. I felt helpless; my limp body was like a rag doll. She leaned me forward pulling the bra straps over each arm and onto my shoulders, and then snapping the hook in the back. *I can see I need easier clothing to wear; this is an ordeal. As a matter of fact, I don't' care if it all hangs out! I'm not going through this hassle. I just won't wear a bra. I can see how men mastered the one-handed bra technique when it came to taking it off!* I silently chuckled to myself thinking about that.

Next Joyce helped me with the T-shirt. She reached for a clean diaper and slid it under me pulling the adhesive tabs at the sides, fitting it snugly on my hips. "This is only temporary, Kate, until you learn bladder control," she reassured me. *I hope that comes back. I feel humiliated having to wear a diaper!* This was the first time I hadn't worn a hospital gown and it felt bizarre. *I'm actually wearing real clothes!* She pulled the elastic waist shorts on and the final step to dressing was the Ted hose. *What are those?* "Everyone has to wear these, Kate, to help with the circulation and prevent blood clots," Joyce said as she struggled to pull them on. *They are hideous looking. These kinds of tights definitely wouldn't run!*

Tennis shoes were placed on my feet, and I was ready for therapy. This was the first time I understood the enormous task and emotional stamina that stroke recovery required. *This is going to be a long, hard road. I can see that.* Joyce was showing me tough love. I certainly wasn't a fashion statement. *I don't care what I look like. I just want to get better.*

My therapists put me on a schedule with rest breaks in between therapy. *I'm ready to do anything to walk again.* The grueling schedule lasted from 9 a.m. until 3 p.m. I had neither energy nor endurance. *I'm a prisoner in my body, completely paralyzed. I can't even move my fingers to activate the call but-*

ton for a nurse. Here I'm totally alone. Panic overcame me. *How am I ever going to get my life back? I have to be willing to do this therapy. It's the only chance I have.*

My second day in rehab continued like an endless SAT examination, therapist after therapist came and went. One of the first I remember was an occupational therapist who entered my room carrying a small black box and a clipboard. *Who is this woman and why is she carrying those items?* The woman was petite with short, cropped blonde hair. "Hi I'm Katrina from occupational therapy. I just need to do an evaluation on Kate," she said. Mum got up out of the chair. "I'll come back after you are finished," she said. "No, no that's fine. I won't be long," the therapist said. *When am I doing the actual therapy? That's what I want.*

Katrina opened the box explaining that she was going to test my joint range of motion. "We need to make sure that's normal," she said. Taking a safety pin, she began pricking my skin in various areas. "Close your eyes, Kate, and tell me if you feel this," she said. *Ouch! Of course, I can feel that!* "Some stroke survivors lose sense of touch," she said while taking notes.

She also tested my muscle strength. She had me squeeze a gadget called a Dynamometer testing my grip strength. "Now, Kate, take this in your right hand and squeeze as hard as you can," Katrina instructed me. I squeezed with every ounce of energy I had. "Really squeeze," Katrina said. *I'm squeezing as hard as I can!* "Good, Kate, I can tell we have some strength there to build on."

The therapist made some comments on her clipboard. "Good, now let's test your dexterity," she said. She raised the head of the bed, sitting me up. She removed some of the remaining items out of the box and left an assortment of colored blocks, which she started to arrange. *I wonder what's going to happen now?* "This particular exercise will give me an idea of your gross motor coordination," Katrina explained. *What is gross motor coordination?* "What I'd like you to do is try to pick up each block and place it in the empty side of the box," she said. *Well that's easy enough! Seems so simple?* "I'm going to give you a minute to see how many you can get in there," she said. *I knew there was a catch! I'm being timed.*

Katrina looked into my eyes for a signal. "Ready?" she said. *Yeah, I'm ready.* I fumbled as I picked each block up trying to put them in the empty side. "Come on, Katie, you can do this," Mum said encouraging me. *I'm trying. I feel clumsy doing this. It's harder than I thought!* "Okay, I think that's good," Katrina said taking some notes. *Well, did I pass? What are you writing? Oh heck this is hopeless!* I started to cry. "You did fine, Kate, don't cry," the therapist said. Mum in a stern voice, said, "Come on, you can do this, pull yourself together. You have to get through this," she said. *I'm trying but I feel so devastated. Look how weak I am!* It was difficult to complete the session without crying.

Another therapist stopped by to do some evaluations. She introduced herself as Delia, and said she was the Physical Therapist. "I'm just going to test lower body strength in your legs," she said. Delia was young and pretty with long hair that was tied back in a ponytail. *She's so young to be doing this kind of work. It's not fair that she gets to go home at night while I'm stuck here! I'm sick of evaluations. I'm eager to begin therapy.* I followed her instructions as she took notes. Her evaluation lasted thirty minutes and she left me to rest.

There was a knock at my door. "Hi Kate," announced this friendly voice. Then I saw this tall slender woman, mid-50s, standing at the foot of my bed. Her head was a mass of tight curls and her smile beamed from ear to ear. She was matronly looking, dressed in a navy skirt, a white shirt with a buttoned down collar and a navy sweater. *Oh, no! She's a nun. She's going to try and convert me!*

She held a folder full of papers under her arm as she came closer to the bedside. "I'm Sister Delores," she said in a soft but assertive voice. "I'll be visiting you for a few minutes each day. I visit all the patients in the ward so you'll be seeing a lot of me."

I just gazed up at her. *How can she smile and complete a sentence at the same time? She reminds me of a schoolteacher I once had.* The Sister touched my arm. "I know how hard it is dear, but you mustn't give up. You have those two beautiful babies to get home to," she said. She reached over me and picked up the photo of my girls. "Oh my, what beautiful girls." *I'm trying to choke back the tears but I feel so sad.* I started to cry. "Oh honey. It's very normal to cry, Kate. That's part of the stroke process. Everything happens for a reason," Sister Delores said. *She's way too sweet and too nice. What does she know about having a stroke? Why did God let this happen?*

Tears were flowing down my cheeks. She leaned closer to my face and squeezed my hand. "Remember Kate, baby steps. God is always with you. He won't forsake you." I looked into her eyes. *I wish I could express to her how I felt. If God is so great, why did this happen? Where is God now?* She placed a little prayer card on the shelf beside me. It was the Lord's Prayer. "I'll see you tomorrow, dear, I have to go now." The sister turned and left the room. Her few words had been encouraging to me. God's word was what I needed to hear and to be reminded that I would heal. After I composed myself, lying there thinking, I knew crying wasn't going to help. *I'm only going to get a red face and puffy eyes from crying. These tears aren't going to help.* Even though I wasn't able to speak, she was there to comfort me and just hold my hand. I did my speaking with my eyes. My inner being with this adversity was deepening my relationship with God. *God is stripping me of everything but I know he has plans for me. I feel so down, so devastated. Why me? Why me? What have I done to deserve this? I feel so alone and helpless. I feel this is the end of the world for me. Life isn't any fun anymore!*

During my rehabilitation at Daniel Freeman Hospital, reading the Bible daily was one of my coping skills that gave me comfort. *God, please give me the use of my legs back. I promise I'll do anything.* Mum would sit with me in rehab and open the stack of cards sent from people all over, as far as New Zealand.

She slowly read each card. Listening to her read what they had said made me weepy. *Doesn't anyone realize I'm paralyzed and it's a struggle to rip envelopes open? I appreciate people thinking of me. I wish I wasn't lying here so sick. No one knows what it's like for me. This is hell!*

At night I was terrified to be by myself. It had been reassuring in ICU to have someone sit with me all night. Here in the hospital I was alone. Steven sensed my fear and spoke with Amy. The evening nurses were notified to play soft music continually in my room. Steven sat with me in the evenings, never leaving until I fell asleep. At 9 p.m. every night, he went to the nurse's station reminding them to administer my sleeping medication. Then he waited until the medication took effect before he would leave. I hated nights. I was eager for morning to come. In the middle of the night I woke up always having the urge to urinate. The catheter had been the first thing to go upon arrival to Daniel Freeman. Learning bladder control was a goal. As a precaution, I was wearing diapers but it was stressed to me to call for a nurse whenever I felt the urge for the bathroom.

I remember one particular evening using every ounce of strength to push the nurse's call button. "Ye–ssss?" I heard coming from the intercom. I looked anxiously toward the door waiting for the nurse. Answering back would have been nice but I couldn't speak and she didn't come. Again using all my strength, I pushed the button. Again I heard, "Ye–ssss?" Frustrated, I wanted to scream through the intercom. *Can't you tell I've had a stroke and can't speak? Please come down here. I need some help.* I kept pushing the button. *If I could speak, I would be complaining to her supervisor. Obviously, I need something if I keep pushing the button. At night this place is a ghost town!*

Finally, the nurse appeared at the doorway. "Do you need something?" she asked. *Yes, I needed you five minutes ago.* It was too late. The damage was done. I couldn't wait. "Do you need the bedpan?" she asked. Walking toward my bed, she grabbed the bedpan off my shelf. *It's too late for that.* Pulling back the covers, she realized what I had been trying to communicate. She gave a heavy sigh. I had created extra work for her. I lay there waiting for her to return with fresh sheets and a gown. *I feel embarrassed just like a small child being scolded. I only hope I can get back to sleep.*

Gradually, over time, I regained bladder control. The diapers were only worn at night as a precaution. (With three or four bladder infections while in the hospital, it made it tough learning bladder control. The feeling of constantly needing to go to the bathroom and nothing happening drove the nurses crazy.) Learning bladder control reminded me of potty training my own daughter. Here I was, learning the basics of life all over again.

I remember being transferred into a wheelchair that first week. Delia, my physical therapist, assisted Katrina. After my self-care session with Joyce every morning, I lay on my bed resting. Just about the time I finished my self-care, morning after morning Steven would walk in. He always made the effort to be in a much better mood than he really was.

The therapist walked in mid-morning, pushing a massive wheelchair. *I hope I'm not going anywhere in that?* The only time I had been in a wheelchair was when I gave birth, and they insist on you being wheeled from the ward to curbside. "Hi, Kate, we are going to sit you up in a wheelchair and take you on a tour of the hospital floor," Katrina said. *I don't want a tour. I feel fine lying here.* The two of them gently transferred me into the wheelchair. *I hate the fact I can't speak!* My body was weak and I had no trunk control. *This feels weird sitting in this.* Katrina situated me in the chair placing a pillow behind my head for support. The wheelchair had a huge back which reclined. She secured a strap across my stomach and snapped it in. *This thing is equipped with a seat belt? What a hassle for a tour of the hospital. I already feel sick!* "If you feel faint from sitting in this position we can recline the chair," Katrina said pushing the wheelchair out the door. Delia followed with the portable tank of oxygen. Steven trailed behind us.

I feel depressed being in this cumbersome wheelchair. Is this what I'll always be in? I started crying. "Oh no, I feel bad. She is crying. Delia," Katrina said concerned. *I'm crying because I'm so discouraged! I'll never get my life back! Why God, does it have to be like this?* "Don't cry. It will get better," Delia said. This was my first tour of the unit. We passed by the therapist's board schedules and the nurse's station. "Now we are going to go and see the apartment," Katrina said. *See an apartment?* I was wheeled down the hallway to a door that opened to a set of rooms like an apartment.

As we entered into the large room, I noticed a couch, chairs and coffee table in one corner. Over in another corner was a small open kitchen with all the amenities. "Each week we have a cooking class where patients can learn to cook again," Katrina explained. There was a dining area complete with a large table surrounded with chairs. "This is something you'll be doing while in rehab," she said. *I don't want to cook. I just want to get better.* "Kate never cooked prior to the stroke," Steven said laughing. Both therapists laughed with him. "Well Kate, I can promise you they won't be gourmet meals, but you'll learn some neat tricks in the kitchen," Katrina said.

Against the wall I noticed a washing machine and dryer. "Kate, here is where patients can learn to do their own laundry from their wheelchairs," Katrina said wheeling me over to it. *What? Do my own laundry? I'm sick and trying to get better. There's no way I'm learning that too. I plan on walking out of here.* Katrina pushed the wheelchair into a room that had a king-size bed. "The bed is used for patients to practice rolling over and getting out of bed," she said. *I hadn't thought about having to relearn that too!*

"Upon discharge patients are given the option of staying over night in the apartment alone or with their spouse to feel what life is going to be like once home. It's safe and located around the apartment are emergency cords to pull if a patient needs the nurse," Katrina reassured me. *I cannot imagine spending any-*

time in that room with Steven. They have to be kidding! She wheeled me into a large bathroom off to the side. I've never seen so many devices in a bathroom!

I know you both mean well, but this is discouraging thinking about having to relearn everything again and new techniques. I feel as if a blanket of sadness has been thrown on me. I tried to choke back my tears, but I started to cry, which quickly turned into a wail. Steven told me, "It's okay to cry, Kate. Let the tears come. This is a part of the mourning process," Delia said. *Look at what I have to face! I can't do this! I hadn't planned on life turning out this way.* I cried as the therapists wheeled me back to my room that had become a safe haven for me. *Why did they have to show me that? It just depressed me more.*

Steven and Mum were with me for my first therapy session. A therapist named Kelly wheeled me to a mat room. Looking back, her jovial attitude was commendable. But at the same time it wasn't the remedy to make me walk or talk again. Weeping, I sat in the chair. *I wish this whole ordeal were over. I'm scared. I feel dizzy sitting up. This is therapy just getting in this wheel-chair!* "It's okay, Kate. Everyone is nervous about therapy in the beginning," she said. "Come on Katie babes, pull yourself together. You can do this," Mum said. *Easy for you to say, Mum, but I'm the one having to do the therapy. I feel my heart racing. What am I going to be doing?*

"Our session will last 30 minutes and then I'll get you back to bed to rest," Kelly said. She wheeled the chair to the edge of the mat. I glanced out the window at the sunny blue sky. *If only this were a dream and none of this was happening. God, just give me the strength to get through this.* (I don't recall the details of that first therapy session but I do remember feeling totally over-whelmed and fatigued. I had no choice but to try and follow her instructions.)

I'm exhausted. I can't even perform these simple exercises. This feels hopeless! When is this double vision going to dissipate? Why does my face feel numb on one side? I wish I could ask

questions. I wish I had answers. I just want to feel better.
Halfway through my session Mum realized how damp my shirt
had become. "Kate, your shirt is saturated with perspiration,"
Mum said alarmed. *Yes, I know. I'm using all my endurance to
follow her instructions. My shirt feels damp against my skin. I'm
exhausted from these simple tasks! What a workout!*

"Kelly, I'm going to get a clean item of clothing. I don't want
her catching a cold," Mum said concerned. *Mum, I don't need a
clean shirt. A little perspiration won't hurt!* "Okay, good idea.
It's amazing the energy it takes for her to sit up," Kelly said. *If
this is how therapy is going to be, I'm not sure I'll make it. I have
to walk again!* Mum returned and Kelly assisted her in changing
my shirt. *I can't even do a simple task like change my clothes!*
After returning to my room, I lay on my bed feeling angry and
depressed. *Why did my life turn out like this? I was so fit and
healthy before this.*

Later that day Mum spoke to Joyce. She expressed concern
that I wasn't getting enough rest and asked about limiting the
visitors. It was decided I would be placed on an up and down
schedule allowing me some rest. This meant after the self-care
session with Katrina, I would rest before my next therapy session. Visitors were limited to ten minutes a day and only after
three in the afternoon. I enjoyed seeing people, although they
were draining my energy. "I'm going to be gone soon and I want
to spend as much time as I can with you. You don't need all these
visitors wearing you out," Mum said. Steven disagreed and he
tried to change the arrangement. I was too tired to fight with
Mum so we adopted her rules. Besides, I had not regained my
speech yet and couldn't speak to her or anyone. I knew I had to
focus on therapy.

My friend Jenny was there the next afternoon for a session of
my therapy. She had politely asked Katrina if she could watch.
Jenny pushed as Katrina walked beside me. We headed to one of
three mat rooms. Then Katrina wheeled my chair to the edge of
the mat platform. Setting the brakes, she helped me up onto the

mat, teaching me to pivot as I turned. *I feel like a limp rag doll.* The wheelchair was an ideal height against the mat for me to transfer. The mat platform was off the ground and made of a wooden frame with a vinyl-coated nylon covering that left enough room for my legs to dangle. The cushy foam padding on the mat made it comfortable for me to sit there.

Katrina urged me to sit near the edge of the mat, placing both feet on the ground for weight bearing. *What if I fall?* "Kate try lifting your right hip and move toward the edge, now try lifting your left hip and do the same movement." *I remember what Sister Delores told me: everything is a baby step. God give me the strength to get through this.* Katrina's goal as a therapist was to help me constantly increase the highest level of independence to apply to my daily living. "We need to work on your trunk control and strength. It's the most important tool you have to work with at this point," she said.

"Sit up straight Kate, squeeze your shoulder blades," Katrina said. She had some plastic stacking cones. "Okay Jenny, stand in front of Kate," she said. Katrina had me reach for a yellow cone and try to grasp it to take the cone out of Jenny's hand. Meanwhile, Katrina laid my left hand flat at my side on the mat pushing in weight bearing. "Try to put weight through this hand," she said. *This is overwhelming trying to think of two things at once.* Katrina sat beside me watching my trunk control. "That's it, Katie. Great job, praise God!" Jenny cheered enthusiastically.

This seemingly simple task was extremely hard and took all my energy. *How can I be this weak?* We tried this for about fifteen minutes before moving onto another exercise. Katrina placed a stool beside me and slightly tilted it. My hand was placed flat on the top of a piece of this odd royal-blue sticky material. The material, dycem, helped secure my hand. This was something I saw the therapists use a lot. Katrina instructed me to try pushing with my left hand while keeping my back upright, shoulder blades squeezed. It took a lot of my concentration. The session lasted no longer than thirty minutes leaving me exhausted. Katrina transferred me back into the wheelchair, and we headed back to my room. "Good job Katie," Jenny said. *You have no idea how hard that was. I feel like I just ran a marathon!*

Jenny stayed in my room keeping me company while I rested. It helped to have a friend there. She had been a good friend, spending numerous afternoons with me in ICU. She had a maternal demeanor with a zeal for life and a love for Jesus. I was hoping God would answer her prayers and give me a miracle. "It's so beautiful outside. We need to get you up, Katie, and take a tour in your wheelchair," she cheerfully said. *Are you sure we should do this? I guess you know what you are doing since your Mum is a stroke survivor in a wheelchair.* I felt comfortable with her. Jenny sat me on the edge of the bed; steadying me as she swung my legs around lifting my petite body into the wheelchair. She propped my feet on each footrest. "At last, Katie, we are ready," she said as she pushed me out into the hallway toward the nurse's station.

She wheeled me down toward the elevator to the ground level and out in the parking lot. *She's right, what a beautiful day. The sun feels good beating against my face. It feels wonderful to be outside in some fresh air. I have missed the warm summer days.* I appreciated seeing the tall trees and plants looking full of life. We headed down the path toward the hospital health center and across their track. Many emotions stirred up inside me as I viewed the hospital health center. I was reminded of once being fit and healthy, able to work out. It was a big part of my life. Now I was stuck in a wheelchair. I started crying. Jenny leaned over wiping my tears on her dress. She turned the wheelchair and started to head back. "Now Katie, that's a true friend when you can wipe your tears on her dress." Jenny's visits stopped with Mum's plan of limiting the visitors. I missed her frequent visits.

Dr. Jeffrey Saver's Comments:

Recovery from a stroke occurs as intact parts of the brain take over the functions of the damaged parts, to the extent they are able to do so. Recent brain imaging studies have disclosed that this shift in functional activity begins soon after a stroke and is driven by training and practice. This activity-dependent neuroplasticity is the biological substrate of successful rehabilitation. Learning to control even simple movements and tasks is an extraordinary challenge to portions of an adult nervous system already committed to other functions. In Kate's case, her youth and excellent fitness before the stroke were factors favoring a good recovery, despite the severe brain injury she suffered. Most important were her spirit and determination. In the crucible of rehabilitation, stroke survivors become stroke victors.

CHAPTER EIGHT

Settling In

my, one of the team members explained her role as a social worker telling me she met with all the new patients. "Kate, I'm here if you need to discuss any issues you may have," she reassured me. *I just need to do some therapy; I don't need psychological help.* "I think it would be good for Kate to see her daughters every day. How have they adjusted with her absence?" Amy asked. "It's been very difficult on them," Steven said. *See my daughters? No, I don't want to until I'm better. I don't want them to see me like this.*

Amy expressed the importance for the girls to see that I was okay. "You will have a life again, Kate, and you'll do many activities with your children," she said. *What kind of activities can I do being paralyzed?* "Kate, I have a daughter about Rachel's age and I can't imagine what you must be going through not being able to see them," Amy said concerned. I started to cry. "I'll try to help you as much as I can," she reassured me. *Try to help? What can you possibly do? I just want to be normal again. I want to get on the floor and play with my kids like other mums do.*

"I think when the girls come to visit, it would be good to have a bag of toys here at the hospital. They can play and visit with Kate," Amy said. "That's a terrific idea, I'll pick up some things today," Mum said. "Kate, you are going to feel like you are on a roller coaster with your emotions. Every stroke patient has a difficult time controlling them for the first few months. This is very normal," Amy explained. *Control my emotions? My life has been turned upside down. This is depressing me more listening to you.*

Amy mentioned that I would probably get close to a couple of the team members during my stay at Daniel Freeman. *There's no way. I have no desire but to work hard and walk out of here. I intend on getting out of here as quickly as possible.*

Families were encouraged to visit. It was decided my daughters would visit me for an hour each day after therapy. I'll never forget the first time Rachel came to see me. Mum asked the nurse to sit me up in the wheelchair. The nurse tried to camouflage the trachea tube by tucking it under my hospital gown. A pillow was propped behind my neck. Mum brushed my hair, letting it flow onto my shoulders. "There you go, Katie, babes," she said. *It still doesn't change the fact I'm disabled. I feel hideous!*

Amy was seated in the room when the girls came. Amanda (the nanny) stood in the doorway holding Rachel with Stephanie beside her. She bent down, "There Rachel, go say hi to mom," she said. Rachel started to cry holding onto Amanda's leg. "Mommy, mommy, pick me up." *I'm your mum, not Amanda! Rachel doesn't even remember me as her mum.* "Stephanie why don't you bring Rachel over to her mom?" suggested Amy. I started to cry. "Don't cry, Mom," Stephanie said, taking Rachel by the hand and coming toward me.

Rachel refused to come too close. She held onto Stephanie's hand. "Sissy, sissy," Rachel said. "It's okay, Rachel, it's Mom," she said. The wheelchair frightened her. *Stephanie is so grown up, taking care of her sister and comforting me. I love you kids very much. I miss you.* Stephanie and Rachel sat on my bed coloring. "Look, mom, I'm coloring a picture for your room. Do you want to help me color?" Stephanie asked. "Your mom can't do that yet," Amy said. *No, I can't even color in the lines. I feel like my life is over!*

Amanda didn't stay too long and was preparing the girls to leave. Rachel reached out and handed me a crayon but kept her distance. *Thanks honey, I wish I could just hold you.* The girls left. "I think it would be a good idea if I got a grounds pass for Kate so the girls can visit her outside. That will be a less threatening environment," Amy said. Everyone agreed. *I don't want to see the girls until I'm better. I feel so helpless. I couldn't even help Stephanie do a simple task like coloring.*

From that point on, the highlight of my day was when my daughters came to visit. Amy managed to get a grounds pass, and I spent an hour visiting the girls each afternoon. Steven and Mum wheeled me downstairs where I would meet the girls and the nanny in the park. We sat under the shade of a huge oak tree. *I'm worried I might have to go to the bathroom. What if I can't get to a toilet in time?*

From my wheelchair I'd sit and watch the girls run up and down the grassy bank. *They aren't even interested in me sitting here. I suppose it shows them I haven't died.* Mum tried taking my mind off the stroke and talking about other things. She took my hair out of the braid and let the air get to it. I just listened as she talked. "You can't always think about your stroke. You need to take an interest in what the kids are doing," she said. *Mum it's hard not thinking about my stroke. You're not the one in the wheelchair. What the heck do you think is on my mind? I just want to walk again. I can't think about anything else. This was a good idea to get a grounds pass. The fresh air feels good.*

My first afternoon in the park I was sitting watching the girls when Rachel came up to me and scratched my arm. *Rachel, that's not nice to scratch your mum. I know you are angry with me for leaving you. I didn't want to honey.* Mum discussed this with Amy at my next visit. "I think it would be good if Kate can transfer from the wheelchair onto the bench so Rachel will feel more comfortable," Amy said. *What's the point? Rachel doesn't see me as her mother.*

Amy's suggestion worked well when the girls came to visit me in the park. Mum had neatly packed snacks for them in the diaper bag and some were put in my lap encouraging Rachel to come over to me. At first she was reluctant. She was afraid of the wheelchair sitting near me. To an eighteen-month-old, it looked like a monster. Gradually over time we got to establish a relationship again.

My bottom ached constantly and Steven would help me stand. "Do you think you should be standing like that without a therapist?" Mum asked. "Ye—s," I managed to get out. *Mum if you had to sit all day in a wheelchair your butt would ache! I just need to relieve the pain.* It felt good as I stood with my arms wrapped around his neck. Mum rubbed my bottom and I wanted to keep standing but my legs buckled under me, forcing me to sit back in the wheelchair

Little things and some big things bothered me. It broke my heart that Rachel thought Amanda was her mother. It bothered me to watch Amanda driving around in my brand-new car. Steven had bought me a brand-new Jeep just a week before my stroke, and now, some stranger was driving around with my kids in the car. Amanda was even wearing my clothes. It made me sad to see this. Even when she bought a Victoria's Secret clothing catalogue for me to look at, it made me more depressed. *What the heck is she thinking?* There were times I would just cry and cry crocodile tears and no one really understood why.

I looked forward to my time in the park after a day of therapy. It was peaceful and small fragments of sunlight shone through the trees. A small squirrel scurried amongst the branches looking for food. Every day like clockwork he'd venture down the tree to see what we had left for him. *I yearn for the day when I have that kind of freedom.* The park was real life. An oasis in the bleak reality of sweet pain and tears; that was the routine of my day.

I was so committed to my therapy that I would wheel myself to the gym just to get five minutes extra of the therapist time. I had trained for years five days a week and I was able to bring that kind of intensity to my rehabilitation. I thank God I was never a couch potato prior to the stroke. In the park I was just a mum, a person, someone glad to be alive.

Amy suggested to my family that I start keeping a journal. *How will that help? How am I supposed to write in a journal!* "What a great idea, Kate. I'll bring one in for you," said Mum. At first the entries were simple, logging daily what I had done in therapy and my progress. (Eventually Amy suggested I start writing in the journal myself. Some of those entries are throughout the book for you to see my early stages of learning to write again. I was right-handed and it meant I just needed to gain my strength back. By writing a few minutes each day, it gradually came back. I didn't feel at the time as if I was making any progress, but looking back over my journal I saw the many miracles I was given.)

I had to learn everything again, from speaking to swallowing, from transferring to a wheelchair to walking. The things we take for granted were difficult challenges for me. One session I remember Delia and Katrina explaining about an odd looking plastic device. "This is called an Incentive Spirometer," she said. *What the heck is that?* "Because of your breathing problems, we need you to try this. It will increase your ability to take bigger, deeper breaths," Delia said. "Using the Spirometer will also keep your lungs strong," Katrina mentioned.

Delia instructed me to breathe into the tube. *I don't want to blow into that!* "Go ahead, Kate, try blowing while I hold this for you," she said. I started to nervously laugh. *I feel stupid blowing into this. I can't do this with you watching me.* Both therapists waited patiently for me to stop laughing. Delia held the device as I tried to blow into the tube. Nothing happened. "Take a deep breath and try blowing as hard as you can into the tube," Katrina said. *See! I can't do it.* Katrina and Delia glanced at each other. "Really try to force some movement of air into the tube, Kate," Delia said. I tried again, this time the tiny ball on the gauge moved barely to two hundred and fifty. It moved a little but I was beginning to feel light-headed from repeatedly trying.

"I think you are exhausted from trying," Katrina said. "Okay, Kate, we will leave this with you, and try to practice as often as you can. Our goal is for you to be able to move the ball to the fifteen hundred level which is normal for a woman's breath," Delia said. *I'll never be able to do that.* "I want you to try and do this every hour for a couple of minutes. Practice at night while watching television during the commercials," Delia suggested. *Yes, that's something I could manage. I can see I'm going to have to make it a priority. Between blowing into this thing and squeezing putty in my right hand to strengthen it, I don't have time for anything else.* "This is something you can do on your own," Katrina said. "It's not part of your therapy, so remember to pace yourself," Delia said. "As you breathe in, try to increase the length and strength of each breath. In order for you to speak, we need to increase your lung capacity," Katrina said. *The words are there but I just can't get them out. Perhaps this will help.* I persistently practiced when I could. I didn't rest. I constantly thought about breathing into the tube. *I have to do this or I'll never speak again. This is my only hope!* Gradually my efforts paid off.

I can remember when I got the luxury of having my first shower. It had been several weeks since I had taken a shower. *When is my therapist going to let me take a shower? I need to have my hair shampooed. My head feels itchy.* "Can't we let Kate take a shower? Steven asked. "Well I'm concerned with Kate's open wounds but I'll check with her doctor," Katrina said. *I would love to take a real shower. I hate these sponge baths.* From the sponge baths, I had advanced to sitting on the edge of the bed with Katrina sitting next to me supporting my trunk. She finally had me advance to doing my self-care from the wheelchair at the sink in my room. This was all a slow process.

When I had enough sitting balance, I was able to start taking showers. After my self-care session one morning we did a "dry-run" as she referred to it. *What's a dry-run?* I was dressed but she wanted to see if I could accomplish the transfer from the wheelchair onto the shower bench in the bathroom. "This is only a practice run. I want to make sure we have a safe environment that will allow enough time for the shower," Katrina said. *But when is the shower? She certainly is cautious!* Katrina wheeled me into the spacious bathroom bringing the chair close to the edge.

"Now there's a 3-inch ledge you'll have to step over, but for now I'm going to help you scoot onto the shower bench," she said, setting the brakes. *How am I going to scoot onto that?* Lifting the armrest on the wheelchair she supported me onto the bench. Swinging my legs around, she scooted my body over more. *Wow! I'm sitting on this thing! At least this bench has a back support.* "I think this will be fine," she said. *I'm disappointed that I can't take a shower today. I have been waiting a long time.*

The next morning, Katrina came in with some tape and plastic. "We can go ahead and try a shower this morning. Because of your trachea and feeding tube sites, we need to cover those with plastic," she said. Cutting pieces of plastic, she then taped over the wound sites. Katrina supported my transfer into the wheelchair. Before wheeling me into the bathroom she put on my tennis shoes. *All this, so I can take a shower?*

In the bathroom she brought my chair to the edge of the shower ledge. Together, we went through the process we had practiced yesterday. Katrina carefully scooted my body onto the bench and brought my legs around. She removed my shoes and gown. "Okay, Kate, try to keep your arm in weight bearing. I want to place your left hand in position so your arm isn't hanging. This way it's getting weight through the arm and activating the muscles," she said. *This is therapy just taking a shower!* Pulling the curtain across, she ran the water.

The tepid water sprayed out at my body. *Oh, this feels heavenly. I have never felt so grateful to take a shower. I'm finally taking a shower! I don't want this to end. There's nothing like a long warm shower.* Tears of joy flowed down my cheeks. "Crying is a normal part of the stroke. It will happen and there's no way for you to control it. I know it must feel wonderful taking a shower," she said. Taking the hand-held shower she wet my hair and began to lather shampoo into my scalp. *That feels good, but how am I going to shampoo my hair myself with one hand?*

"Okay, Kate, I think we had better finish here in a moment. I don't want you to get tired from the steam," she said. Turning the water off she began to dry me while I sat on the bench. She carefully dried my feet and put my shoes on. "I don't want you slipping," she said, drying the floor. She laid towels on the floor. *There's no way I'd slip with the amount of towels you have scattered on the floor. Oh this must look like a sight! Tennis shoes and nothing else!* Loosely covering me with a gown she transferred me into my chair and wheeled me to my sink area. I sat in my chair as she dressed me.

Katrina explained the technique I'd be using for dressing. "Remember, Kate, as you dress you will be crossing your weak leg over your good leg." *I have to remind myself of that too? All of these techniques that I have to learn, it's overwhelming! How am I going to accomplish dressing with one working hand?* "As you undress, you have to reverse the process. Start with the weak side of your body," she said. *How am I going to remember everything?* Katrina assured me it would get easier. "This is as hard as it's going to be. Remember, as you are getting dressed we want your arm in weight bearing and not just in your lap," she said.

(Weight bearing meant that my hand would support my body, improving the tone thus allowing me to learn to balance myself. There was a sense in which you could say that weight bearing was the key to my new life! *If I can learn this, the sky might be the limit for me.*)

Getting my chance to be fitted with a new wheelchair felt great. I remember when Delia arrived in my room to transfer me into the wheelchair taking me by the apartment. "I think you are ready for a new wheelchair Kate," she said. As we turned the corner, I saw a row of wheelchairs lined up. Delia walked down the row looking for the right wheelchair. *I feel like I'm being fitted for a pair of shoes.* Unlocking the chain she pulled one from the line, "I think this will work." The wheelchair was certainly smaller with no headrest. This was called a quickie. It seemed easier to manage. The chair was comfortable with a cushion behind my back and bottom. We wheeled toward the mat room. *This will work. I like it already.*

After therapy Katrina informed me a doctor was scheduled to plug my trachea. "This is exciting Kate. No more trachea tube and no more breathing treatments," she said. I was scared and excited at the same time. The breathing treatments were not going to be missed. Every four hours a respiratory therapist would come to my room. For twenty minutes I would sit with a mask on over my face breathing in short quick breaths keeping my lungs clear.

I remember a female doctor coming to my room. I was scared, very scared. "It's okay, it means you are getting better. You'll be fine," the doctor said. She could sense my apprehension, and she calmed me down. The procedure was quick, painless, and I was left with a red plug in my trachea. I looked in the mirror. *The white bandage around my neck with this red plastic plug looks like I'm wearing a bow tie. Somehow I've kept my sense of humor.* It was wonderful not having this tube dragging from my neck. I had practiced my breathing trying to cough up on my own. I had been worried that having the trachea tube removed meant I wouldn't be able to breathe on my own. *Now I no longer have to cover the tube to take a shower!*

Over the next few weeks my routine did get easier. I had progressed to standing and sidestepping into the shower. My dressing techniques became easier and Katrina assisted when needed. I felt clumsy attempting to dress, but I didn't give up. *I'm not going to give in to this stroke.* I remember the process of side stepping over the ledge. This was a small ledge to step over, yet it was so hard for me. I was now wearing an air splint brace to give my leg support. Before wheeling me into the bathroom Katrina put the brace and shoes on.

"I want to make sure we protect your ankle," she said. *Am I always going to have to go through this process each time? This seems like too much work!* I wheeled my chair to the edge of the ledge. "Okay, Kate, come to a stance and reach with your arm for the grab bar," she instructed. I leaned forward getting out of my chair and faced the wall. I grabbed the bar and waited for her instruction. Katrina secured a gait belt around my waist.

"Now as you move into the shower stall, you will be shifting your weight back and forth on each leg. Follow along with my instructions and take it slow. I'm going to stabilize your knee so it doesn't buckle," she said. I listened to her suggestions. "This is going to be the biggest challenge for you to step over this ledge. Go ahead and lift your right foot remembering your weight should be on your left side. Steady now. Try not to be impulsive," she instructed.

Katrina assisted lifting my left foot over the ledge, as I gradually eased myself down, reaching for the shower chair. "Good job, Kate. The team has talked about a fitted brace being made for your left foot. The AFO will help to give more stability to the ankle," she said. *Wow! I made it! I've been successful, at least this far. That was exhausting though. I didn't realize how tough that would be.*

A weird looking device was made for my hand to be in weight bearing. The "dome" splint fitted over my left knee with a piece of dycem on the top. My hand lay on top, activating the muscles in the arm. *Thank goodness I only have to wear this in the hospital! I wouldn't be seen in public with this on.* I recall watching the splint being made. The powder-like substance was heated in a frying, pan allowing the therapist to mold the material which then created an instant hard surface.

At this point, each day was unknown. There were days that nothing happened and then there were days when a muscle that had been flaccid would suddenly twitch.

Rachel's rendering of "Kate's Journey"

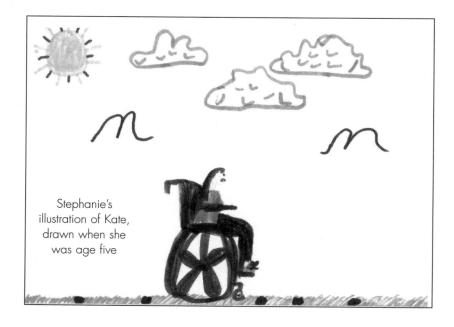

Stephanie's illustration of Kate, drawn when she was age five

The following are taken from the personal journal Kate had kept while going through her ordeal.

8-10
UPGRADE PILET
TO SOFT
did test ~ SPO quest
more standing
leqning on elbows

Kate Kuynos

8-1f

Stevens birthday
took some steps
knelt on knees

wheelchair mobility
standing

writing

lunch group

Kafe climymen.
1210 8th st
MB
Cal 90266

8-19

It's saturday and
very quiet
i don't like the
weekend
I pray for a micro
on my left eye
did some more
standing transfers
and went to the
park w/ kids
had dinner
on a reg
diet
think liquids

hard workout
took more
steps
worked on
keeping
shoulders back
tube
wound good

8 / 23

much easier to
get dressed
put bra and shir
on by myself
did a cooking clu
and ate the lunch
fett alfredo, bread
rolls, and choc
mousse pie

felt tired today
my muscles are sore
have to have help
always got to let

9-2
had accident in the
toilet. Steve- forgot
to pull my pants
down. We laughed so
hard

9-2
had my shower
then worked out for
an 1½ with Deb,
UJ some am work
There is movement in
my elbow and
bicep. saw Sharon &
Roh with everyone
in the park.
had dinner
and rested.
   some vistors
Barney
Terry
Jenny
Still weak on left
side but each
day is better

8   9-14

I took my shower &
went swimming first
which went really
well. I was able to handle
myself better. I then did
some PT with Delia and
showed Steven some
steps. It was then time
for lunch. I was late &
as usual the last to finish.
But I then had OT at 1pm
where I went down to out
patient and did some arm
and a little standing.
Nina helped me with that.
It was a good session
I came back & had a 30
minute rest before heading
to PT at 2.30 which I did
stretching and leg
movements. Finally at 3pm
I rested then the
kids came and we
went to the park
with Cheryl

10-6

Its Friday and I have
one more week here. I
cant wait to leave,
they have alot of
patients and not really
that much time for
me. It seems I'm too
healthy now!
I was suppose to have
swimming - I got ready
and Candice didn't show.
Then I got really upset
beause I couldn't get a
nurse to help me. They
were too busy. Denise
my nurse helped me to
shower and I worked
on the arm for an
hour. Candice came to
apologise. I did therapy
and then lunch.
after I lay down for
an hour and rested.
I then did some more
therapy until 3pm

CHAPTER NINE

Speaking of Eating

t was wonderful to walk, see and hear, but nothing could match the joy I began to feel once I could communicate, especially with my children. The first tentative primitive steps had begun in ICU where I had been given simple mouth exercises that taught me to make strange sounds through my passé-muir value. No one would make any promises that I would recover and speak again. Steven continually gave me hope giving me encouragement that I would fully recover. In rehab he had fresh flowers delivered every Friday, knowing how much I loved flowers. I never knew if they meant I would be getting better or if this was the week I would be having my funeral!

At Daniel Freeman I had a special caring woman who helped me learn to reach out and touch the outside world with my own ideas and words. Norma, a speech pathologist, who was tall, slender and wearing a white medical coat was that woman. Amy was right. I would bond with a couple of people. Besides Steven and Dr. Kolodney, Norma was my next most devoted fan. I could tell Norma expected me to get better and her faith was contagious. It helped me so much.

Norma was worked into my regular schedule spending an hour or so with me a day. It was her job to teach me not only to speak again but swallow and drink. I remember sitting in my wheelchair and Norma handing me some pen and paper asking me to write my name. *Sure, this is no problem.* To my surprise, my name looked like a chicken scratch! I was devastated. Norma reassured me that with practice it would get better.

Norma's good nature made me feel at ease. Whatever home-work she left with me, Steven would see to it that I did it again and again. They were a powerful team. He made a large sign in his own handwriting hanging over my bed instructing the nurses on how to use my speech value. Even though the sign was up, he discovered on one occasion that the value was not properly shut off. I was about to pass out when he started screaming for help. If he had not been around, I could not have screamed for help. I would have suffocated in a few more minutes and died. I was thankful there were non-medical people around me at all times.

Norma prepared me for eating again with a special powdered solution called "thick-it," which made thin liquids lumpy and easier to swallow. My speaking was coming along but I had an awfully hard time learning to swallow again. There was some fear that I would never be able to drink liquids again on my own. Norma had a lot of faith in me and kept working. Finally after a few weeks of work a very important day came. I was going to get a special test to see if I could swallow on my own. I would be seated in front of an X-ray machine and photographed as I swal-lowed liquids of different viscosity.

A technician came into my room and transferred me onto a gurney. He raised it so I was at a slight angle. *I'm nervous. This is the big moment. I feel like I'm going for a driver's license. Please don't let me fail!* I was wheeled down to speech pathology. "I'll be back to wheel you upstairs after the test," he said. Norma encouraged me in a soft voice, "Kate we have practiced for this day and I know you are ready. If you pass this test, you'll be able to start eating solid foods and we can get rid of the feeding tube." *I want to pass this so bad.* "Let me sit you up a little more and place a pillow behind your back. Comfortable?" she asked. I nodded my head. *What's going to happen here? I'm nervous. I hate not knowing what to expect.*

"This is a relatively easy test, Kate, and there's no pain. It's very quick and involves taking some pictures and eating," she said. *I haven't eaten for so long, I can't wait.* Norma explained the procedure to Steven, motioning him over to a small room with a window. I could see him standing behind the tinted glass. He had a look of trepidation on his face, standing there with his arms folded. *I wish I wasn't doing this. Calm down, you can get through this.*

"Okay, Kate, let me show you what I've prepared," Norma said approaching me. "This is pureed applesauce mixed with a thick gooey paste substance called Barium. It's totally harmless and shows us what's happening on the X-ray. We like to start with this so you won't aspirate," she explained. *What is aspirating?* Luckily for me Steven asked Norma. "Aspirating is when you do not swallow the food and instead you let the food go into your lungs. It's what we mean when we say food went down the wrong pipe," Norma explained. She scooped a small amount of Barium from the paper cup. *That's the eating part of the test? I had visions of actually being able to eat something.*

"I want you to take a portion of this and hold it in your mouth until I tell you to swallow it," Norma said. She cautioned me to go slow taking my time. "Okay, here we go, Kate, ready?" she asked. I opened my mouth to take the applesauce, and then Norma ran back to the screen. I panicked. *Hurry up; this won't stay in my mouth. I'm going to swallow it.* This seemed like an eternity to me. "You can swallow now, Kate," she called. I was able to tolerate the pureed applesauce only slightly coughing. "Good job, Kate, we can move onto the next item," she said. Steven could see the whole thing on the screen. He saw the food enter my mouth; my esophagus open and watched the food go into my stomach.

Norma now filled a teaspoon of liquid from a paper cup. *I would give anything to have a large glass of water! That's not even going to wet my whistle as Mum used to say.* "I want you to swallow a little of this, but wait until I give you the cue," she reminded me. "Okay, here we go, Kate, ready for this?" she asked. I held the liquid in my mouth while Norma ran back to the screen. *I hope you hurry because I feel like I'm going to swal-*

low it. "Now Kate," she said. I swallowed on cue, immediately aspirating. I started coughing; my whole body shook violently.

Steven horrified by what he saw came running out of the room. "Kate, are you okay? I could see the liquid shoot right into your lungs," he said. Norma followed behind him. I was not in great danger or at least as Steven understood it. I had just courted pneumonia, the number one killer of people in my condition. From the exam room I was wheeled to X-ray. I spent about an hour in the radiology department. Steven could not believe what he had seen. He had no idea if I could breathe or if I would get pneumonia or what just happened. Finally I was brought out to the hall with Norma beside me.

"What just happened Norma?" he asked. Norma explained, "Kate, did fine with the thick liquid, but the thin liquid slipped straight into her lungs. We proved she can eat certain kinds of foods and she does have a primitive swallow reflex. I'm going to recommend she be put on a diet of pureed food." *Pureed foods? I haven't eaten for weeks and all I'm getting is a teaspoon of applesauce?* "We will try this test again later but for now I recommend a diet of pureed food, which will allow her to begin tasting things again," she said.

Norma felt confident having all my foods pureed. This would be safe and allow me to have the feeding tube at night. Eventually this would lead to my being able to have the G-tube removed. (I didn't know it at the time but some people never learn how to swallow again, never having the G-tube removed.)

"Absolutely no thin liquids for Kate. She can't tolerate them," Norma told Steven. *I'm not going to have liquids at all?* He looked at her curiously, "How long will it be before she can eat regular food?" He was anxious for me to eat. "Kate hasn't eaten for weeks. Can't we let her have something?" he pleaded. "We need to stay with the pureed food and in a week or two we'll do another evaluation. Maybe after that we can try thin liquids," Norma replied hopefully. Noticing I was teary-eyed, she patted my hand, "Oh Kate, you did great. I'm just very cautious." *You may be cautious, but I had hopes of being able to eat again. Now I can't even have a glass of water! I've failed this test!*

Norma again explained what happened to me, "Kate, your liquids are going down the wrong way but you are able to tolerate the applesauce okay, because it is heavier than water. Let's hold off on any thin liquids right now." *I was looking forward to drinking water.* "Let me illustrate it like this; if you take a cup of water and pour it on the floor, it moves really fast and breaks apart, not holding together. But if you compare that with a cup of honey and do the same thing, it moves slowly staying together. You have weak muscles in your neck right now and the liquids are moving too fast through your body. That's why I want you to stay with everything pureed," she said. Steven agreed, "Yes I can see why." *I understand but I'm just disappointed.*

The technician came to wheel the gurney upstairs. "Bye Kate, you did fine," Norma said. *Not as well as I would have liked.* "Well, how did it go?" he cheerfully asked. "Not as good as we hoped," Steven interjected. "Oh you'll pass with flying colors next time. Very few patients pass the evaluations the first time," he reassured me. *I feel embarrassed failing this test. Now everyone in rehab will want to know how I did.*

Norma instructed Steven to make sure a family member was present at meal times. At lunch Norma would sit in my room helping me to eat. She showed my family what to do, encouraging me to sit in the wheelchair, making the food digestion easier. (I remember those first sessions when I was spoon fed the pureed food like a baby.)

A white hospital towel was draped around my neck to catch any food. As I gained strength I fed myself. Sometimes I missed my mouth with the pureed food landing on my cheek. It was frustrating, lifting my quivering hand with the teaspoon to my mouth. "Don't worry, Kate, that's why we have the towel, so take your time," Norma cautioned. *This is frustrating. It must be boring for them all to watch me eat. I just hate this!*

"Slow down, Katie babes," Mum reminded me. Norma sat with me for about a week observing me and then suggested that I might enjoy entering an eating program. I could sit with others who had the same swallowing problems. Everyone was enthusiastic to have me join the eating group. *I don't want to be eating with others. I just want to go home.*

"Kate, you'll meet others with swallowing problems and it will get you out of this room," Norma expressed. *I'm probably going to be the youngest person too!* "I don't feel comfortable leaving you by yourself. In the lunch room a therapist is there to observe the group," she added. "I'll leave directions for nurses in case I'm not around.

A note was taped to my closet door giving strict instructions about swallowing. The sign read: **Kate is to take only small, bite-size portions, finish each bite, and put her fork down in between each bite. All liquids should be thickened—no straws!** At the time these seemed like harsh rules but I realized they were for my benefit. My food trays never looked appetizing, consisting of pureed turkey, mashed potatoes with gravy and pureed carrots. *This is disgusting! I never eat this stuff.* About the only part I liked was vanilla custard or chocolate pudding. I always requested two of those.

Steven could not believe I could eat this food, and yet I ate every ounce I was given. *I need to eat to get better. No matter how bad this looks or tastes I have to force myself to eat. I don't have a choice.* Life was just so hard at this point. Nothing was easy or fun. Eating was a major ordeal. It was humiliating for me to have others watch me. Mum continuously tried to sound encouraging, "You are a fragile wee thing, you need the energy. Come on Katie, eat up." She helped prepare my tray by taking off cellophane from the containers. "Looks yummy, Katie, even pureed turkey on your plate." *I do want to get better, I've always been health conscious and watched what I ate. I guess I'll have to eat this if I want to improve. I can't imagine anyone else eating this food.*

During the day I was free to get a juice from the rehab dining room. I couldn't get enough of the nectar base juice. It wasn't long before Norma gave me permission to start using a straw to take small sips of liquid. "You are the first patient, Kate, that I have ever let use a straw this early. I trust you and think you are ready," she said. *Wow! That's another miracle I have been given.* Gradually, I was upgraded to a soft mechanical diet and before the end of my discharge I was allowed to eat solid foods again with caution. Every morning I started my day off with a delicious piece of cheesecake that Steven brought me. He was amazing. It seemed like there was nothing too small or too big that he couldn't do for me. Steven had given up everything to care for me.

On Tuesdays, the rehab team met with the neurologist, Doctor Alexander, discussing each patient's progress and goals for the following week. Amy discussed those with me and I looked forward to hearing what they were because it gave me something to work toward. *Baby steps, Kate, just keep taking baby steps.*

I was nervous and I didn't know what to expect when I attended my first family conference with the rehab team. My family wheeled me into the room where the team members and my doctor were seated in a circle. *It feels weird sitting in here and hearing everyone talk about me. I hate this!*

Each team member gave a brief evaluation of my recovery. Doctor Alexandra explained that he was pleased with my progress. Katrina reported that she had been working on the activities of daily living. "I want Kate to incorporate her left arm into her activities," she said. (Even today I must sit on the edge of the bed to dress. Standing is not an option.)

Delia shared how pleased she was with my progress. "Kate is a great patient to work with and willing to do the therapy," she said. *What choice do I have?* Steven asked, "Well, are Kate's left arm and leg going to come back?" Delia took a deep breath, "We certainly hope so, but I can't say for certain. Sometimes we have to trick the muscles into working and we are doing everything we can to facilitate what does come back. As she improves, hopefully, we can use less and less equipment." *I hope so, please let me walk again and be able to use my arm. I have to get the use of my arm back.*

Joyce expressed some areas of concern. "We have put water back into Kate's diet during the day so she is not wanting it at night. There is a risk of pneumonia because of immobility," Joyce said. "Is that something we need to be concerned with?" Mum asked. "No, because when she is moving and coughing more the risk is decreased. That is a common problem with most patients," she said. "What about these leg spasms? Mum asked. *Yes I hate those and they scare me.* "I think over time that will get better. If we give Kate drugs for that, it will slow her recovery," Joyce explained. *Forget it then!*

"Kate is doing really well and is very cooperative. She no longer needs cues about her swallowing and is able to use a straw. Liquids are very important to prevent pneumonia," Norma said from speech pathology. "When can she have thin liquids?" Steven asked. "I'd like to keep her on thick liquids for a while. When her coughing and throat clearing is not a problem, then maybe we can try thin liquids," she said.

The case manager Desiree finished out the session discussing her role with the insurance company. "I'm speaking with the external case manager on a weekly basis regarding her progress, goals and length of stay," she said. "I don't want Kate leaving until she is medically ready to be discharged," Steven said. *You don't have to stay here. I want to be at home.* "There will come a point when her progress will slow down and the question will be, is twenty-four hour care going to be needed? Would Kate's needs be better met at home? These are questions we can address in our next family conference," Desiree said. *This is depressing hearing them talk about twenty-four hour nursing care? I have to get better!*

"Daniel Freeman doesn't have a contract for outpatient therapy so she may have to choose another facility," Desiree said. *What is she talking about?* I sat in my wheelchair listening to everyone feeling more depressed and becoming tearful. *I feel hopeless about my situation. I'll probably always be in this wheelchair!*

───ᴍ──ᴍ──ᴍ───

The time came for Mum to go home to New Zealand. *I knew I was going to dread this moment, Mum.* "I'm sorry but I have to get back. You are in good hands now," she said. *But Mum, I don't want you to leave. Please don't go.* I started crying. She put her arms around me, "I don't want to leave you honey but I have to. You know how much I love you. My plane leaves this evening and I need to pack. I'll call you before leaving the airport." As she walked out of the room I started sobbing uncontrollably.

"Bye honey," she said wiping her tears with a tissue. *Damn! I can't stop crying. I've become used to having her around. It really saddens me to see her leave. I wasn't going to get this upset.* Steven called Mum from my room prior to her leaving for the airport. He held the phone to my ear. *I can't get any words out.* I sobbed into the earpiece. "Kate, say something. I have to leave honey. Are you there?" she said, *Yeah I'm here. I can't stop crying to get any words out. I don't want you to leave me.*

Sobbing, I gasped for air. Mum finally hung up the phone. *Why did you put me through that Steven? I couldn't say anything to her. I'm too upset. I spent the evening feeling depressed. I don't want to see anyone. When will I see her again?* (Mum has since told me that she could hear my sobbing down the hallway.) "I will hear your sobs until my dying days. How I got on that plane, I'll never know," she told me. I haven't seen Mum since my rehab days.

CHAPTER TEN

Moving On

eeting recreational therapists seemed a total waste of time. *Why do I need recreation therapists? I'm paralyzed for Gods sake! How am I supposed to do anything fun?*

"My role is to get you to do some of the activities you did prior to your stroke," Caroline said when she was introduced to me. *Activities I did prior to the stroke? I'll never be able to do those.* I was resistant to the idea of working with her. She explained to Steven some activities I could begin to incorporate into my life again. *This is a total waste of time!*

"What kind of activities did you like, Kate?" Caroline asked. *Things I'm certainly not going to be able to do now. My life will never be the same!* I tried to hold back my tears. Listening to her made it worse, wishing I wasn't in this position. "Kate was very active before her illness," Steven said. "Hopefully we can replace some of those activities with something you can do," Caroline said. *I just want to walk again and get out of here.* She discussed options for me while I was staying at Daniel Freeman Hospital. She talked about community outings, going to movies, and restaurants and incorporating car transfers.

The first time I met Larry, another recreational therapist, he really annoyed me. He came into my room after visiting a much older patient in the next room. Speaking extremely slowly, but so loud he could have raised the dead, he said, "How are you? My name is Larry and I'm a recreational therapist." *Larry I'm not deaf! I'm not the patient next door. I'm a young 33-year-old who can hear perfectly. You don't have to yell at the top of your lungs!*

Larry visited patients in the early evening encouraging us to get up and see the magic show, which took place in the dining room every Tuesday night. I had already nicknamed him. *Oh here comes Loud Larry Magic and his traveling show! I'm too tired for this. I would consider it if a magic wand was waved over me and I was healed.* I never did go, mainly because I was exhausted from a day of therapy. I just didn't have the energy.

The first time Caroline wheeled me into the chapel I broke down sobbing. "There is a service on Sunday mornings and a therapist can bring you by," she said. *I don't care about a service. What's the point?* Caroline slowly wheeled the chair toward the altar. I sat there sobbing. *Why God? Why did you let this happen to me?* "It's okay, Kate, this is a natural response," she said touching my shoulder. *Just get me out of here?* I waved my arm toward the door. I wept loudly as she wheeled me out. *I don't want to come back here!*

—⚏— —⚏— —⚏—

Holidays are the loneliest times in a hospital. I will always remember Labor Day holiday weekend that year in the hospital. The staff usually tried to have some kind of celebration to gather the patients together. That weekend is still just like it was yesterday. The area was decorated and there was a barbeque for us. *I would rather be outside with friends and family.* Larry and Caroline had organized some activities for the patients. There was an activity for our hand coordination skills. A blown-up paper target was pasted on the wall.

We lined up behind each other in our wheelchairs waiting for our turn. *We look like we're lining up for a derby. This is dumb! Aiming with a water gun to squirt that? This sure is a labor of love from Larry.* As easy as it sounded some patients struggled to hit the target. I was the next one in line. "Okay Kate, just aim and shoot," Larry said. *Oh yeah, I'll aim and shoot.* I held the water gun up and instead of hitting Larry's target I aimed right at him, and creamed him. Chuckling to myself, I kept squirting at him even faster. Larry held his hands up defending himself. In good humor he laughed, "Your motor skills are working." At least this brought a smile to both our faces.

The remainder of the afternoon was spent with family. It depressed me listening to patients at the gathering complain about what they could and couldn't do. I would have preferred spending the afternoon doing therapy. Lying in my bed early that evening I cried tears. *Nothing was fun today. For a split second I had fun squirting Larry but otherwise this whole thing depressed me! I hate being disabled.*

For some of my therapy sessions, Steven wheeled me to the mat room so I didn't have to wait for a therapist. As I grew stronger I wheeled myself to the sessions. *Having him bring me here does save time.* Therapy was a process of baby steps and slowly I could see the miracles. Over time I started doing exercises that felt more beneficial to me. There was a range-of-motion exercise where Delia had me lie down on the mat, and then one of my legs was placed on a powder board, allowing me to move my leg without much effort. (The powder board was raised off the ground approximately seven inches with four legs. The therapist sprinkled talcum powder, thus the name, over the board so it was easier for me to move.)

With the use of the board I could slide my leg back and forth, which lessened the impact of gravity. Steven cheered me on, "Good job, Kate. Now keep trying." *You have no idea how hard this is. I really have to concentrate on moving my leg. Keep kneeling right in front of me; you are the perfect target.* "Come on Kate. Really try to kick me. You can do it," he said. With every ounce of energy I moved my leg and to the surprise of him and the therapist my leg flew forward. *Oh my God! My leg just moved.* Steven quickly got up. "Wow, Kate, you just missed me," he said smiling. He was holding his hands over his trouser fly.

Let's try that again. That was fun. Maybe this time I'll actually kick you.

Everyone in the gym fell apart laughing, we all just collapsed in laughter. It felt so good to laugh. Steven pretended to collapse in a mound. It was all good fun. *It makes me realize how hard the man is pushing me. He can really frustrate the heck out of me!* Steven did not care. He didn't care if I hated him or loved him. He just wanted me to walk again.

CHAPTER ELEVEN

Raising the Bar:
From Here to There and Back Again

R ehabilitation was hard work and a constant challenge. My muscles were constantly sore and I was in agonizing pain at the end of each day. *I need something stronger than aspirin to help. I find the routine to be exhausting. I'm determined to bounce back from this misfortune!*

I remember the morning Delia had me try to walk with the aid of the parallel bars. I was wheeled over to the bars. "This is something we use to check your gait pattern," she said. *I've wanted to try these.* Delia placed the brakes on my chair and stood behind me supporting my torso while Steven held my left hand firmly on the rail. She adjusted the bars so they were waist high for me. "Don't worry, Kate, I'm right here. Try to remember your hip control and gradually bring your foot through as you take a step," she said. *She makes it sound so simple!*

"We have you, Kate, you can do this," Steven said. Slowly I took a step forward, bringing my other foot through. *That felt awkward. I feel like I'm lifting a dead weight.* "Take it slow, Kate," Delia cautioned, "Let's try that again and really focus your concentration. We are right here with you," she said. *I'm trying to remember everything you have told me. If I go any slower, a turtle could beat me!*

"Stand up tall as if you are being pulled by a string. Remember to hold your stomach in and squeeze your shoulder blades. Don't forget to breathe," Delia said. Step by step I moved along the mat at a snail's pace. Droplets of sweat formed and began to trickle down from my forehead. We hadn't gone far when Delia thought I should sit down. "Can you bring her wheelchair behind her? I think she is becoming fatigued," Delia said. *I feel as if my legs are going to give out. I need to sit down.*

Steven wheeled the chair onto the rubber mat and Delia supported me as I sat down. *Ahh! That's a relief to sit down. I can't believe how exhausted I feel. My first attempt of using the parallel bars is pathetic.* "I think we would do better at this exercise once Kate has her brace. It will give her the knee support she needs," she said. *But I want to be able to use the bars!* My session on the parallel bars was over.

With the decision the team had made for my brace, a cast of my leg was done for the fitting. The brace will make it easier for you to walk, Kate," Delia said. "It will help with the foot drop and knee control," she told me. *Is this something I'll always have to wear? Can I wear this with shoes?* Delia noticed the look of fear in my eyes. "Don't worry. The ankle-foot brace is designed to fit inside your shoe. We are hoping this is a temporary thing. In the meantime we will continue to work on your walking in therapy," she said.

I vividly remember that morning when I was fitted for the brace. I was nervous when Delia wheeled me to a therapy room to meet the orthopedist. I was firmly seated in my wheelchair, brakes on. *I wonder how this is done?* "Hi, I'm Mike. *So,* we are going to fit you for a brace," he said. *He makes it sound so simple.* Mike started preparing his things. I sat there intensely watching him. He had hands of a worker, reminding me of my father. A film of white dust covered his clothes. "Just sit there and relax," he said, spreading a white sheet on the floor. Mike crouched down and slipped a knee high pantyhose on my leg. He used his ink pencil to mark the various spots on the panty hose. Down the center of my leg he ran a long thin piece of plastic. *Wonder what that is for?*

He soaked the plaster bandages in the tepid water in a basin next to him and then gently wrung them out. Unraveling the bandages, he wrapped them evenly around my foot and leg up to my knee. Like a potter at the wheel, his hands flowed cautiously caressing the plaster, smoothing it out. He had a rhythm as he worked his hands, which were covered with the thick, gooey white mixture. Slowly the plaster hardened, and again he marked the cast with an ink pen. He ran a knife down the center to pry the cast open. *That's why that plastic is there!* Mike used some cast spreaders to open the cast, gently easing my leg out. I was left with a thin white layer of plaster on my leg, which he carefully rubbed off. "I'll be back next week with your custom-made brace," he said. "Thanks, Mike, I'll see you later," Delia said as she released the brakes on my wheelchair. *Wow. This will be wonderful to help me walk.*

When it came time to try my new brace, Delia eased my foot in. It felt firm. "The brace will help provide support. We will still work on strengthening your weak muscle. The brace will protect your foot from rolling," she said. I stood up out of my wheelchair and held onto the bar. "This will help with the foot drop you have," Delia said. I slowly took a step bringing my foot through. *I think this will prevent the foot from dragging although it feels weird.* The brace, AFO, as therapists refer to it, was made of plastic and came up to my knee. At the top there was a buckle that a strap went through. *I suppose if this will aid me in walking, I have to live with this ugly looking brace!*

The rehabilitation process was slow. Results, although they were satisfying to others, were not nearly fast enough for me. *I have had lots of miracles, I've regained the use of my right side, my double vision is dissipating and I'm eating pureed foods. Little by little my speech is coming back. I do have a lot to be grateful for but I want to be how I used to be.* It was Erma Bombeck who wrote, "If life is a bowl of cherries, what are we doing in the pits?" *That's for sure! Life feels like the bottom has fallen out of the barrel and everything has caved in. I feel as if I am on an emotional roller coaster all the time.*

Some days I felt great and could see progress; others I was so depressed. Getting through therapy was a struggle. Learning how to tie tennis shoes was hard. *How can I do this with one hand? I loved shoes prior to my stroke.* "Kate you need to learn to tie your own laces. Let me show you the one handed way," Katrina would tell me. *There is no way I'm going to learn that. I won't need to know because I'm getting the use of my arm back. No, I'm fine as long as someone can help me. I don't want to learn that.* "No," I said. *God has given me a second chance at life and now is not the time for a pity party; I have work to do.* Each day upon awakening I would pray that God would give me the strength to make it through the day. With God's help I gave therapy 100 percent for three months one day at a time.

Remember Psalm 116:8—*I have delivered your life from death, your eyes from tears, and your feet from stumbling and falling. When you need relief, come to me in spirit and truth and you will find it.* This Psalm gave me much comfort.

I have never prayed so much in my life as I did during this time. Prayer is very powerful. "It's only for a season," Sister Delores would tell me. My room was full of scripture that Sister Delores taped up each week. *Well, let the season be over soon! Life is full of ups and downs but I believe it is how we react to the adversity that molds our lives. I have been delivered from death's doorstep; for that I'm grateful.*

I'm reminded of the story about the teacup. The refiner's fire was so intense that the teacup screamed, "What are you doing to me?" But it was the fire that made the cup into a beautiful work of art. God was molding the teacup into something exquisite. Just like the teacup I was forced into a pottery oven of circumstances, trembling and afraid. I discovered there was nothing I could do but stand there and burn until God delivered me from death to life. I believe God has been molding my life as the Bible says, "Trials come to test our faith to produce in us the quality of endurance."

CHAPTER TWELVE

Happy Birthday Mr. Klugman

*I*t was a beautiful August day and I could hardly wait for our planned picnic later that afternoon. It was Steven's forty-eighth birthday, August 14th. He and I and the children had been through so much since that awful day of June 29th. We were ready for some celebration. I awoke that morning excited about the picnic in the park. I had my usual therapy session. After lunch I was advised that I would not be receiving any more therapy today. *What is happening now? Why am I not having therapy?*

A sign was attached to my door; **QUARANTINE: NO ONE IS TO ENTER WITHOUT SPECIAL PERMISSION.** Nurses started wearing gowns, rubber gloves and masks around me. *What is going on? What could be wrong that I have been quarantined? Everyone around me seems to be genuinely frightened. I feel like an alien or a monster from the Blue Lagoon. I wish Steven were here to sort this out. I'm being totally ignored.*

Steven arrived at his normal time to wheel me downstairs to the park. Like clockwork he showed up each day in the morning for therapy until lunchtime and returned at three o'clock in the afternoon for me to see my daughters. Amanda took the girls to the park while Steven came to my room to get me. I looked forward to our routine each day. Today he was excited about celebrating his birthday in the park. Upon his arrival, he was shocked to see me in quarantine.

Now, on the verge of hysteria he strode to the nurses' station with this newest problem. It was just one too many for him! He had the doctor paged to find out why I was quarantined. When Steven returned to my room he was wearing a gown, mask and gloves. *What the heck is going on?* "What– is–going–on? I- want- to- see- the- girls- to-day," I said taking short breaths as I spoke.

"Kate, I'll get to the bottom of this," Steven said. *I feel like an outcast with everyone wearing this stuff around me. I hate this!* "Don't be scared. We have been through so much together. I cannot imagine this being too serious," he said.

Who is he kidding? No big deal! The whole hospital has stamped leprosy all over my room! No big deal? Then why is everyone wearing special clothes and treating me like I'm a character in an Alfred Hitchcock movie? Now he is wearing protective gear! What is wrong with me?

Finally, Steven reached the doctor, and learned the reason for the quarantine. It seems I had brought the infection over from Torrance Memorial Hospital. This kind of infection had never been seen at Daniel Freeman. Everyone was concerned the infection could spread throughout the hospital killing hundreds of patients. After running a culture test it turned out that my feeding tube was growing the same deadly pseudomonas bacteria I had in ICU. The infection was resistant to all known antibodies. No one knew how to kill this bug or how far it could spread.

The doctor explained, "Pseudomonas can't grow in the stomach. The natural acids kill it. Kate is in no danger but at this point; however, we can't remove the tube until we have looked into this."

"I would feel more comfortable if the tube was removed. This is awful to put her through this," Steven said. Trying to put on a happy face, he remained calm but I could tell he was shaking with fear. *Some Birthday party this is going to be!*

Putting the medical staff on trial, Steven demanded an infectious disease specialist be called, but the staff had beaten him to it. Steven questioned at length the infectious disease specialist, the internist, lung specialist and speech pathologist. He was convinced I no longer needed the feeding tube. Confident that I could make it without the tube, Steven insisted it be removed immediately. Forcing a staff meeting, the pros and cons were debated. The doctors wanted to be sure I could take in enough food on my own.

"Okay, turn the tube off today and let's see how she does," Steven said. He felt the risk of having to feed me by IVs was not as bad as the risk of having me die of a bacterial infection. The doctors were reluctant. They explained the surgical procedure for removing the tube, which was not as straightforward as Steven had hoped. He feared the procedure could spread the infection, and instead of an infected feeding tube, he would have an infected wife. Nevertheless, he demanded that the feeding tube be turned off, and asked that I receive all nourishment from pureed foods. Steven wanted the deadly feeding tube removed the next day. Once again it was he against the medical establishment. Nothing was done that day.

But Steven had a plan, which he did not let me in on; and I had no clue until it was over. Presenting himself bright and early the next day at the nurse's station, he informed the nurses that he wanted a surgeon called immediately. "I want this feeding tube removed now, right now," he firmly said. A red circle of infection was appearing around my belly button. Steven was not going to wait a moment longer.

The nurses told Steven nothing could be done. They agreed to make a note on my chart. "Nonsense, you could get someone here in five minutes if you wanted too. I intend to stay here until a surgeon is called," he said. He stood waiting patiently, arms folded across his chest. "Mr. Klugman, we simply cannot call anyone from here. I'm sorry we can't help you," Joyce, the head nurse said.

"I just want to save my wife's life. It's up to you people. Can't you help me?" he pleaded. No answer.

"Okay, hand me a phone book and I will call a doctor myself. I'll get someone here to perform the procedure," he said.

"You cannot do that," Joyce said.

"The hell I can't!" Steven yelled.

Luckily for Steven, the nurse on duty that day was a substitute from the nurse's registry, and she supported his decision. "This man is trying to save his wife's life. Why don't we help him instead of fighting him?" she said, handing Steven the phone book.

Steven began thumbing through the yellow pages randomly calling doctors. Joyce, letting out a sigh, finally grabbed the phone book back from Steven and placed a call. Within fifteen minutes, a surgeon arrived, who was prepared to perform the procedure.

Steven explained his concern about the procedure spreading the deadly infection. "Oh don't worry about that," the doctor said. "What do you mean?" Steven asked.

"Pseudomonas can't live in the stomach. There is no chance the infection can spread. The acids in the stomach would kill any bacteria," he said.

"Good Lord! Well why did they put us through this? I have been going through hell and now you tell me it was all for nothing?" Steven said.

"I don't know. Anyway, don't be alarmed. This will be over in less than an hour," the doctor said.

Steven came to my room telling me the news. I was taken by gurney downstairs. A nurse reassured me everything would be fine. *I hope you are right.* I felt a needle go in to sedate me. "You should start to feel groggy in a moment. When the pain medication starts working the doctor can begin," she said. She left the room and I was alone with silence and my thoughts. I lay waiting. *I wish this was over. What am I going to feel?* Steven waited patiently outside.

Before long, a doctor came in. "Okay, Kate, this will be over before you know it," he said, putting gloves on. *Just start. I want this thing out!* The procedure was quick but the pain intense. *Oh God, I thought I wouldn't feel anything? I can't take this! Please let this be over. Why can I feel what he's doing? I feel like I'm going to throw up. Something is being ripped up through my stomach. I can feel the tube being pulled! Is this coming out through my mouth?*

Just when I felt I couldn't stand the pain, I heard the doctor. "Okay, Kate, it's out," he said. *Thank God! I feel light-headed from this.* I lay exhausted on the gurney while I was wheeled back to my room. "Good job, Kate. Now you have slowly gotten rid of these tubes," Steven said, relieved. *You have no idea how intense that pain was.* Somehow I lived through it.

I glanced at the clock on the wall. It was 2:45, and I usually saw Delia for my 3:00 therapy session. "C-a-n - y-o-u - no-ti-fy - De-l-i-a - I-want - to - keep - my - ther-a-py - ap-point-ment?" I said.

"But you just had surgery. I think you should rest," Steven insisted.

I feel okay. Besides I wasn't given that much pain medication. I can do some therapy from the bedside. I don't want to miss my therapy. I have missed too much.

"G—o," I motioned, waving my hand.

"You're not the only stubborn person in this hospital," he muttered leaving the room.

Sheepishly, he informed Delia of my desire to do therapy. "Yes, I figured Kate would want that. Kate is so determined. I have never seen anyone so determined. I have some exercises we can do with her from the bed," Delia said. At my bedside she gave me some simple range of motion exercises requiring little effort. *I'm glad I managed to keep my therapy appointment. I will do anything to walk again! I can't miss therapy, even if it is from my bed.*

Dr. Jeffrey Saver's Comments:

Stroke patients are at elevated risk for a variety of medical illnesses. Loss of control over swallowing increases the chance of bacteria entering the lungs and causing pneumonia. Prolonged bedrest fosters the formation of blood clots in leg veins and of skin breakdown. Tubes into the lungs, stomach, and bladder allow bacteria to migrate past the skin and cause internal infections. In the past, most stroke patients died from one or another of these medical complications of stroke. Modern supportive care is designed to reduce the risk of developing supervening medical illness, but they remain a common cause of setback and distress in the rehabilitation process.

Chapter Thirteen

Cooking On All Burners

My therapists began to include the rehab-cooking group as part of my therapy. I had finally met the criteria for being able to eat real food and began cooking classes on Wednesdays. My diet was soft food. Katrina's goal for me was to become self-sufficient in the kitchen. *I never cooked prior to my stroke so why would I want to put myself through this agonizing process? How am I supposed to cook with one arm?* The first time I was wheeled to the apartment, I thought I was going to be the only one in the kitchen. To my surprise there were six other patients. *How the heck are we all going to move about in this tiny kitchen? I thought this was going to be a one-on-one session.*

All of us were at different stages in our recovery. A couple of us were in wheelchairs, some on walkers and canes. Katrina briefly introduced me to everyone. *I don't want to be here with everyone.* "Kate, you will be situated at the counter incorporating standing while you are preparing food," she said. *How can I think of two things at the same time? This doesn't look like as much fun as I thought!*

I waited patiently in my wheelchair as Katrina organized each patient. *This is going to take forever to make something! We all move like snails.* Katrina situated a couple of the patients at the table who had trouble standing. "The best part of this therapy is that you all get to sit down and eat the meal you have prepared," she said. *I'm not sure I want to eat anything I've prepared!*

The task I was given was to make chocolate pudding for dessert. *There's nothing to chocolate pudding! That's easy.*

I remember my first attempt making the chocolate pudding. To speed the process Katrina attached the beaters to a handheld mixer. She then turned them to medium speed, and I began mixing. Suddenly, the attachments to the beater came off, and the pudding mixture went flying through the air and landed everywhere. Lumpy globs were sticking on things.

Oh my God! What a mess! If I had an extra hand, I could grab those. Well, I'll try and finish what I started. What is the point of cooking if it's going to take this long? Everything is therapy. At least the bowl had a rubber ring on the base to secure it. Having the use of both hands would have made this easier. My, how I've taken things for granted!

In the beginning Katrina helped by opening the pudding box and I used my teeth to rip open the packet. Unfortunately most of the powder mix would land on me, so very little went into the bowl. What normally took five minutes to prepare took me an hour.

"Don't forget your posture, Kate," she reminded. *Don't forget my posture? How about the pudding that's everywhere?* The next challenge was to pour the pudding mixture into individual bowls. *An extra hand would help right now. It takes me twice as long to prepare anything with only the use of one arm.* Katrina held the bowl at an angle as the mixture sluggishly poured into the bowls. She scooped out the remaining pudding and put it in the fridge to set. Making chocolate pudding became easier and less messy each week. Katrina would situate my wheelchair behind me so I could sit if standing became a problem. She gave me constant reminders on my posture. *I know, I know. Squeeze the shoulder blades and hold my stomach in. Push weight through the weak arm.* "Pretend you have a hundred-dollar bill between your butt cheeks," she said laughing. *I'd really be squeezing if I did!*

Since my weight was really down, eating chocolate pudding became a favorite. Steven daily brought me a favorite treat of cheesecake, and with my self-prepared meals, I was eating four chocolate puddings. Needless to say, eventually both had to stop. The dietician changed my eating plan to low fat.

After we cooked each meal, we sat down and ate it. The worse part was cleaning up. That was therapy too! Over lunch Katrina discussed with us what we were going to cook that next week. Diet plans were taken into consideration. She jotted down the ingredients and went grocery shopping the week prior to the class. "It has to be something healthy and include a job for everyone." she stressed. Those of us who could speak certainly voiced our opinions on what should be cooked.

Ultimately the final decision came from Katrina. I offered to make fresh fruit salad with strawberries and kiwi fruit. After that I was known as the "kiwi girl," making weekly fruit salad. Everyone at the table would start laughing at my meal suggestion. "Oh no, Kate, not the fruit salad again," Katrina would say. (I haven't made a strawberry and kiwi fruit salad since!)

Making fruit salad with one arm isn't easy! Katrina helped me to peel the kiwi fruit and I sliced them using the chopping board with a couple of stainless steel nails in it. The nails made it easier to steady whatever I was chopping. I washed strawberries, slicing them and put them in the bowl. The chopping board was great. It is often a topic of conversation for anyone who comes into my kitchen today, because it has allowed me some independence in the kitchen.

Weekly meals rotated between pasta, stir fry and lasagna. Preparing these simple meals was a huge task for anyone with physical limitations. All of us required naps after lunch. Cooking was exhausting. I became very social as my speech improved. New patients to the group often asked, "What happened to you?" No one could believe I had suffered a stroke at such a young age. (I didn't realize at the time, but this is a daily question from people I meet now.)

During lunches Katrina made a point to go around the table and have each patient say their name and why they were in the hospital. This gave us the chance to know each other and also an opportunity to practice speaking. Some patients took a long time to complete a sentence due to their speech problems. I fought back the urge to finish the sentence for them. We sat patiently letting each patient express themselves. The cooking group helped me realize we all had different limitations but one goal in common: to get better. I could clearly speak the best of anyone in the group, but my cooking ability left a lot to be desired!

One afternoon while I was resting, Amy stopped by. I appreciated my time alone with her, and felt safe enough to tell her anything. "How was cooking today?" she asked. "Good but exhausting," I replied. Amy listened as I expressed my fears and concerns about the transition to home and being with my daughters again. "I want to feel closer to the girls," I told her. "You will. It will take time. Try a fun activity like blowing bubbles with the girls," she suggested. *That's a great idea. They love blowing bubbles.* "I like that idea Amy," I said. "It will also help you with your breathing and your speech. The girls will feel their mom is doing something fun with them. All kids love blowing bubbles," she said. *I'm finding myself taking a breath between each word. Perhaps this will help.*

"I have a more positive attitude about my wheelchair. I can see that it will enable me to get around and not be a hindrance," I said.

"For right now, Kate, it's a necessity," Amy said. "You will be discharged from the hospital soon, and it's important for the team and your family to discuss your needs. The hospital allows you to stay in the rehab-apartment overnight prior to your discharge to see if there are any remaining aspects to address. You are familiar with the kitchen now," Amy said.

Spending time in the kitchen has never been my thing. I don't have a desire to stay in the apartment. I'm already overwhelmed just learning to walk. I'm sure I'll be fine. I'm definitely not staying in the apartment. I just want to be home in my own bed.

"Well Kate, you sound like you are ready to go home," Amy said. "Yes, I'm looking forward to it. There's so much I want to do to get my house in order." I said.

"Just remember when you do go home to take it slow. It's going to be an adjustment," she reminded me. She left me with that thought.

I became more comfortable with rehab. Wheeling myself around the hospital floors I would often cross paths with Sister Delores in the hallway. Sister always spurred me on, "You can do it Kate! Way to go! Far Out!" she'd say. She always had a smile on her face matching her bubbly personality. "Good job!" she said. It would make me chuckle hearing the phrases come out of her mouth. I had never met a nun like her. She had a real bounce in her step. "It's baby steps, Kate," she'd remind me. *That's true, but it's not fast enough for me! I want to walk.* Sister was always affirming and positive, believing I would have a miracle.

Joyce grew on me. She encouraged me to yell her name out if I needed help rather than pushing the nurse's button. "Don't push the button, Kate, strengthen those muscles and yell for me," she told me. Joyce was right. My vocal cords were healthy but weak. I needed to develop volume. I no longer was that quiet timid person. She constantly urged me to strive for independence. My answers to questions had been a simple "yes" or "no." Speech had been painfully slow and distorted. By practicing breathing and talking more, my sentences became longer.

Therapists could hardly keep up with my endless requests for information. "Did I do okay? Will I ever walk again? How long will it be before I can walk?" It was imperative for me to know. "You did great Kate, you have to work at it," I was repeatedly told. I was determined to get better. I asked Delia what kind of exercises I could do from the bed. "Well, Kate," she said. "Try to practice bridging." *Bridging?* "Lift your butt up squeezing, hips raised high. Hold it in that position for a count of ten, then repeat," she said. This I could manage. It was an exercise I was familiar with having had the bedpan slid under me. The therapists hesitated to give me too many exercises. They could tell I was determined to get better but wanted me to relax. "Don't overdo it Kate, you need to rest," they'd say.

Typically I had the same routine each day. At 7:00 a.m. an attendant, Thomas, came to my room to wake me. Helping me transfer into my wheelchair, he wrapped a blanket around my shoulders and wheeled me to the dining room. Part of my therapy was eating with six others around a circular table. Patiently we had to wait while Thomas placed our carefully prepared trays in front of us. Towels were draped around our necks. In the beginning I found the group meals hard just like my cooking sessions. I had to master opening a small carton of milk by prying it open with the fork end.

Breakfast and lunch meals were eaten with the group. I was the youngest stroke survivor in the group. Miriam Brown, a dear lady in her late 80s, always insisted on extra napkins as she ate. Miriam and I became close and continued our friendship when we were discharged from the hospital. She loved my daughters and treated them like her own grandchildren. Christmas, 2000 Miriam died. Then there was Pedro, a Spanish man who spoke no English; so conversations with him were out. We had a petite Asian woman whose daughter came every morning to assist her. Pearl, in her 60s, was assisted by one of her sons. She was blind from her stroke. Paul, an attorney in his 40s, had been a runner prior to his stroke. Now left in a wheelchair, he managed to amuse the group with his dry sense of humor. Finally, Mr. Parker, who was in his eighties, really disliked being in the hospital. At night he could frequently be heard yelling from his room, "I want to go home." Because of our swallowing problems, a speech therapist observed us as we ate, paying particular attention that we didn't pocket any food in our mouths.

CHAPTER FOURTEEN

Continued Progress
and Goals in Rehab

Another team conference was arranged so my brother and sister could take back information to my parents in New Zealand. Lynn and Tony were present along with Steven and me. I remember that afternoon with each therapist giving their reports of what they were working on. Amy busily took notes. Norma mentioned, "I would like to recommend two or three weeks of speech therapy. Kate's breath support has improved and she is better at speaking and vocalizing sentences. She remains on thick liquids slowly incorporating regular solid foods into her diet."

Delia said, "Kate's mobility has improved immensely since she was admitted. At the moment she needs 25 percent assistance moving in and out of bed. We are going to begin family training. In terms of equipment, we are looking at keeping her present model of wheelchair and a quad cane that has four feet on it." *I'm glad I'm keeping this wheelchair but I could do without that ugly cane.*

Steven was curious about a couple things Delia had mentioned. "What exactly is the procedure for family training? I'd like Kate to remain here and get as much therapy as she can. Is that possible?" he asked. *Are you crazy? I am sick of this place! I want to go home. You don't have to do the grueling therapy.* "I'm sure she is eager to get home. The family training is designed to help you feel comfortable with the wheelchair transfers and getting her in and out of the shower and any needs she may have," Delia answered.

Katrina gave her input, "Kate has improved from needing cues in the beginning to being able to sit on a bench and take her shower. She needs help standing, but her dressing is with minimal assistance. Her movement in the shoulder is good; however, predictability of arm return is not presently known." *I have to get the use of my arm back.* Amy noted items that I would need in the home. Listed were grab bars, a hand-held shower hose, shower chair, non-skid rubber mat and a bedside commode. "Someone will need to get these for her. As far as the family training, we can start to work on that," Katrina said. *I was hoping I wouldn't need those items, especially the commode!*

The meeting briefly ended with Larry from recreational therapy saying, "Kate is currently doing sedentary activity in the pool once a week. She's showing good progress there," he said. *Sedentary is right! But I do look forward to the water even though it's a hassle getting in.* "As part of her therapy one of our goals is to include a therapeutic community outing each week. We feel Kate is ready and has enough endurance to go on an outing," he said. The team agreed. *Where am I going to go looking like this?*

I discussed my concerns and anxieties about the upcoming outing with Amy in my next session. "What if I start laughing uncontrollably?" I asked. "Don't worry, just enjoy the outing, the laughing is part of the stroke. You can't help that, Kate," she said.

I remember Katrina asking me if I would welcome an outing to a local restaurant. "How about lunch at the local Sizzler?" she asked. *What could possibly be therapeutic about that? Heck no. I want to go shopping.* "Katrina, I like the Sizzler restaurant but for my first community outing, I'd love to go window shopping at Nordstroms," I told her. Katrina laughed, "Okay I'll see what I can arrange." The team discussed the idea and thought about ways to incorporate therapy into the outing. It was arranged. I would be going to the mall.

Caroline and Larry drove me to the mall. In the van were a couple of teenage boys from my cooking group, who were also paralyzed. They weren't stroke survivors; both had accidents while riding motorcycles. They rode in the hospital vehicle going to the mall as part of their therapy. *Why do they have to come? Guys don't like shopping!* Larry securely strapped each wheelchair in the van. *Wow! This is an ordeal just for a shopping trip.* We patiently sat as he pulled the straps taut. *Now I really feel disabled sitting like this in a van for handicapped people.*

Caroline sat in the back explaining some of the goals. "I would like you, Kate, to work on some standing and even utilizing the bathroom in a public place," she said. *I thought this was supposed to be therapeutic. I don't plan on going to the potty.* The van pulled out of the Daniel Freeman parking lot. *Finally, we are leaving.*

Steven wanted to be there for my first outing and followed the van in his car with my brother and sister. This was the first time I had driven in a vehicle, and I felt extremely nauseated on the journey. *I can't wait to get there. When are we going to get there?* Thirty minutes later Larry pulled into the parking area where I looked up, and to my dismay saw we were outside the wrong department store. *Mervyn's? This is the wrong end of the mall. Why are we here? I want to be outside Nordstroms.*

"Caroline, why are we parking here?" I asked.

"Well, this is part of your therapy to wheel yourself through the mall to Nordstroms," she said. *Oh great! I knew she would make me work. How embarrassing. People are going to stare.*

People did stare, probably because there were three wheelchairs with young people in them and five people walking beside us. *What's the matter? Haven't you seen someone in a wheelchair?* I pushed myself with my good leg. Happily I looked in the shop windows. I was glad to be out of the hospital setting. Larry and the two boys went to the food court area.

"Do you want me to push you, Kate?" My sister Lynn asked. *That would be wonderful. I'm already exhausted.*

"She's fine, this is part of her therapy," Caroline said. *No, it's your way of torturing a poor disabled woman.*

I was wheeling past Victoria's Secret and decided to go in. *Wouldn't it be great to wear something sexy again?* Caroline and the others followed. I wheeled around the store. Pushing a wheelchair on carpet is a nightmare!

"I'll buy you anything you want," Steven said. *How sweet but nothing is going to look good on me again.* I found it difficult maneuvering the wheelchair between the display tables. *Why the heck are these tables like this? Don't these people understand this is hard for someone disabled?*

The display tables were beautifully arranged with flowing cloths draped over them. Stacks of neatly folded bras and panties lay on top of each table. *These tables look nice but I feel like I'm in a maze. Being in a wheelchair I never saw it from this perspective before.* As I was wheeling past one of the display tables, my wheel caught an end of the display cloth. The cloth slowly started twisting in the wheel. Suddenly I felt something heavy dragging along with me.

"Oh, Kate, hold on," Caroline said laughing.

"Stop, Kate, stop," Steven yelled. *What?* The lingerie items fell to the floor and I turned red when I realized what happened. *Oh my! Well if I didn't want to be noticed before, I surely am now.*

An assistant came rushing over. "Don't worry. I'll fix this," she said.

"Sorry, I'm learning to drive this thing," I said laughing. Steven apologized profusely explaining that it was my first outing into the community. Lynn quickly wheeled me out of the store.

Lynn and Tony could be heard laughing as we wheeled toward Nordstroms.

"That was classic," Tony said laughing. Entering the store, I headed straight for the makeup counter to my friend Donna who was shocked to see me in a wheelchair.

"I wondered where you were," she said. *I feel embarrassed seeing someone I know.* It was nice catching up with her and she gave me a quick make over. *Wow! I feel terrific! I'm not going to wash this off.*

"You look like a new woman, Kate, I'm sure you are tired. We need to head back," Caroline said. *I feel like a new woman. I realized something today, as long as I can write my name and pull a credit card out with one hand; I'll be fine.* In order to save time Caroline briskly pushed my wheelchair. *Now you want to push me!*

We met up with Larry and the boys. "Wow, Kate, you look different," Larry said. *Yes I feel good.* I left my family and returned to the hospital. Larry began the process of getting each of us in the van. *I wish I was going with my family.* The outing had been an experience that left us exhausted. The day ended with an early dinner and bed. Tomorrow was a new day and more therapy.

A couple of days later Katrina explained during my self-care session that I was going on a home evaluation.

"We have scheduled a home outing as part of your therapy. Delia and I need to visit your home to make sure it's a safe environment for you. We need to make sure you can function in your own home," she said. *Does this mean I'll be going home soon? I don't want to go home to visit.*

The therapist and I arrived at my house and Delia pulled into my driveway. *I feel apprehensive about being here. I never thought I'd see this day. I can feel my heart beating fast.* Delia assembled the chair and wheeled me to the front door where everyone greeted me.

"Mommy, Mommy," Stephanie said throwing her arms around me. *I wasn't prepared for the kids and the dog. This has been turned into a production!*

"Are you coming home today?" Stephanie asked. "No honey, I'm only here for a couple of hours," I told her. Delia explained to her that the house needed to be safe friendly for me.

"Oh okay. Look mommy, Jenny is glad to see you," Stephanie said dragging the dog by its collar. *Oh Jenny girl, I miss you too.* "I kept the girls home from school today because they wanted to see you, Kate," Steven said excitedly. *I love see-*

ing the girls but I need to concentrate. "Everyone was excited about your visit and Amanda has been up since 5:00 a.m. cleaning," he said. I glanced around. *Everything looks neat and tidy. I can't believe I'm inside my house again. Feels like I've been on a long vacation.*

Delia and Katrina walked around my house making suggestions. My eyes searched around the living room spotting things that upset me. *This is cluttered looking! I never kept a house like this. My plants look dead and there are crayon marks everywhere. This doesn't feel like my home. I've been gone four long months.* "These throw rugs will have to be put away so you don't trip," Katrina said. *I love my rugs on the floor. It's going to look so bare.* "That's not a problem. I can remove those," Amanda said.

"Okay, Kate, let's have you stand and try walking with the walker," Delia said wrapping a gate belt around my waist. I leaned on the walker and in a clumsy way headed toward my kitchen.

"Think about lifting your left foot, Kate, instead of dragging it," Delia said. *I'm doing the best I can.* I fumbled trying to step up onto the tile floor. *This is only a three-inch step. I can't believe how hard this is!* I stood still catching my breath gazing around my kitchen that was once so neat and tidy. Sheets of yellow legal paper were taped above my stove listing instructions and phone numbers. My counter tops were scattered with odd items. *Nothing looks organized and this is her idea of cleaning?*

"Kate, we need to stay focused on your walking," Delia said. *I know but this is the first time I've been home and I want to see how everything looks. Oh, I wish I could fix everything how I had it. I can see how difficult adjusting to this is going to be.* I turned the walker, taking slow steps. *Oh my! Even Rachel is growing up before my eyes. She's sitting in a booster chair now?* The high chair that sat in the kitchen corner was replaced with a brightly colored booster seat. *I feel so weak and overwhelmed right now. I need to get healthier before I tackle this problem. The house is going to have to wait. Priorities!*

"We will also need to put a couple of wheelchair ramps in for her. The house is a relatively open space, but she'll still need those," Delia said. *But my beautiful hardwood floor! My house is being rearranged so I can move around in this hideous chair! I plan on walking out of the hospital. I feel depressed listening to you.*

"Before any patient is discharged, we have to visit their home. This is routine, Kate," Delia said. (Two portable ramps that only required a piece of non-skid material under each end were installed.)

The therapists suggested that I only use the downstairs portion of my house. Katrina took a quick look around the rest of the house. "I can turn this den into a bedroom for Kate and there's a small bathroom she can use," Steven said.

"I think that will work fine, although there's no reason why she can't sleep upstairs at night," she said. *I agree with you. I don't want to be down here by myself. I would rather sleep in my master bedroom.*

"I want to sleep upstairs. Can't you carry me upstairs at night?" I asked. "No, unfortunately I have a bad back," Steven replied. *Forget about your back. I've just had a stroke.*

"What if I need help?" I asked.

"I'll get you a tiny bell to ring, and Amanda or I will help."

A bell? What if no one hears me? This is going to be scary not having nurses nearby. What does Amanda know? She's here for the kids.

"We need to make sure her wheelchair can fit comfortably through this bathroom door," Delia said.

Katrina measured it. "This will work but it's tight. Try wheeling your chair through," she said. I managed to fit through the door and had barely enough room to comfortably wheel up to the shower door. "Okay good. Next let's try a dry run on seeing how you will transfer into the shower. I need to measure where the grab bars will go," she explained.

Grab bars? My beautiful shower tiles will be ruined. I can't put grab bars in here! I wish I didn't need all these adjustments. I feel like I'm very old.

Setting the brakes on the chair, Katrina assisted me as I stepped over the tiny ledge. Standing in the shower, I held onto the window ledge to balance myself. Inside the shower stall came the kids and dog. *This is crazy! I can't handle kids and a dog in here. It's too small.*

"Remember, Kate, you will have a shower bench in here to sit on," Katrina said. She measured where the grab bars would go.

"Please take the kids and dog out. I can't concentrate," I said annoyingly. *I need to remain calm. I don't want to get upset.*

Katrina smiled, "That's how it is with kids, and you'll have to get used to that. You haven't been around them and I'm sure they miss you." *That's true. It's going to take some time getting used to them, Steven, the dog and my disability. I feel like crying. I'm so depressed.* I choked back my tears realizing that crying wasn't going to help anything. The girls, along with Jenny, were guided out.

Katrina and Delia finished taking measurements and prepared me to go back to the hospital. I sat in silence on the way back thinking of how my life used to be. Upon returning Joyce asked, "How was your home visit?"

Distressed I answered, "Depressing. Nothing is how I used to keep it. All my house plants are dead as well."

Joyce replied, "Kate, you'll be home soon and can have people help you organize. Right now you have to focus your energy on getting better. There's no point becoming agitated." *I know she's right. There is nothing I can do but it still depresses me. I can't wait to go home.*

That evening as Steven sat with me, we talked about my visit home. "Are you going to be okay going home not quite 100 percent?" he inquired. *Not quite a 100 percent? Are you saying I'm not going to walk out of here? I haven't looked at it like that. But now I realize that when the therapists were talking about ramps, that meant that I'm going to be stuck in this chair! I'm going to be leaving the hospital in a wheelchair.*

"What choice do I have? I must have faith I'll walk again. I refuse to believe otherwise," I said.

"Well, just don't give up, Kate," he said. *Amy is right. Going home is going to be an adjustment!*

Another home outing came on a Saturday afternoon. Once home I rested on the couch watching everyone around me. The den was being rearranged for my arrival home. My neighbors, Rocky and Doreen, came over and offered the use of a hospital bed that had been sitting in their living room.

"Dad just passed away this past week and you are welcome to use it before we return it," Doreen said. *I don't want to sleep in a bed where someone had just died!*

"Great, I'll take you up on that offer," Steven said. All three left to bring the bed over.

I transferred into my wheelchair to go outside to watch. *I guess this will work. Besides someone would have died in those hospital beds I used in ICU and rehab. It's a weird thought but I never looked at it like that.* Steven and Rocky wheeled the bed down the street. It was quite a sight. It fit perfectly into the den where I was going to sleep. The remainder of the afternoon was spent resting before my return to the hospital.

Another common consequence of stroke is emotional lability. In one form, this can manifest as increased emotional reactivity, with the patient feeling intense sadness and happiness in response to relatively minor stimuli. Another form is termed "pathologic laughing and crying." Interruption of the brain pathways that exert control over the motor crying and laughing can disinhibit expression of affect. Individuals may weep or laugh too easily and too intensely, out of proportion to the degree of internal sadness or happiness they feel. Sometimes they may even have mood-incongruent facial displays of affect, crying when they are happy or laughing when they are sad. Fortunately, these conditions tend to improve with time after stroke, and can often be helped by specific medications.

Dr. Jeffrey Saver's Comments:

Strokes can affect emotions in numerous ways. Nearly half of all stroke patients experience a period of depression following their stroke. In part, depressed mood is a natural reaction to the sudden alteration in life circumstances stroke brings about. In addition, brain lesions can directly compromise the neurotransmitter systems that underlie mood, producing depression by altering the brain circuitry of emotion.

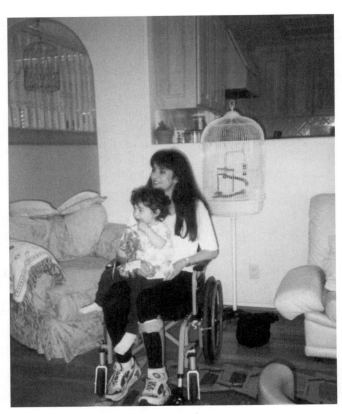

Kate back at home

CHAPTER FIFTEEN

Returning Home

had mental images of what it would be like to be at home. Numerous days were spent lying in bed, dreaming about being home. And now, I couldn't believe that day had arrived. Home had been a magical word; images of being with my daughters constantly flashed through my mind. On October 15, 1995, I was going home. I was ecstatic but apprehensive. *Is this really going to happen?*

My girlfriend, Cherri arrived early Saturday morning to help me pack. Discharge was scheduled for 10:00 a.m.

"Where's Steven?" I asked.

"I don't know," she replied puzzled. *He knew I was coming home today. Where the heck is he?*

"Okay, Kate let's get started. We can do this without him. I don't have a lot of time," Cherri said. She had three or four cardboard boxes with her. I was astonished at all the things I had accumulated over the past few months. Feeling helpless sitting in my wheelchair, I watched as Cherri started packing my possessions. Diapers, bandages, diaper rash cream, a roll of toilet tissue, a bottle of lotion, and a couple boxes of Kleenex were put in a box.

"I don't need those," I said in a determined voice.

Cherri said, "You paid for those items, Kate, these are yours."

Hesitating I asked, "Are you sure Cherri?"

Laughing she said, "They will be thrown away anyway." *I don't care if I ever see that stuff again.*

Cherri loaded the two carts up, flowers and all. A nurse helped her wheel one of the carts down the hallway. I followed, pushing myself in the wheelchair with my strong leg. As we headed down the hallway, Steven was walking toward us.

"Oh, you've finished?" he asked in a surprised tone. *Great timing.*

Cherri was quick to answer, "Yes, but you can still help. Here, pull one of these carts."

He took the handle and started pulling. "I was exhausted and overslept. I wanted to hire a crew to clean the house. But Amanda assured me she would stay up all night and get the house sparkling; however she completely failed me. I was busy getting things ready," he said wearily.

I know why you were late this morning, but your lateness has hurt my feelings. I said nothing. Once downstairs in the parking lot I watched as the boxes were put in the car. *At last I'm going home! I really am going home; this is it.* Steven wheeled me around to the passenger side of the car assisting me. *I wonder if he remembers how to do a car transfer?*

Katrina had given him sessions on wheelchair transfers. I felt more comfortable with Katrina transferring me. Steven managed well and I sensed his nervousness. *I can't say anything because I know he's doing his best.* We drove out of the hospital parking lot with few words being exchanged on the ride home. I was eager to be back in my own home.

That afternoon Cherri helped me settle into my new surroundings. The girls came running into the room excited I was home. "Mommy needs rest girls, don't bother her," their dad said.

Stephanie and Rachel started bouncing on the bed. Stephanie holding the control panel started pushing the button to make the bed rise. "Look at me daddy," Rachel screamed excited.

"Don't let them play with that; it's not a toy," I said frustrated. It was a strain to get the words out.

"Stop it Rachel. Stop it," Steven said harshly. Both girls kept bouncing on the bed, neither listening. *So much for the peace I had dreamed of!* "They are glad to have their Mom home," he replied.

"Come on girls, off the bed, I need to make that," Cherri said walking into the room holding some sheets. The girls jumped off the bed and ran outside to play.

Cherri made the bed with the new sheets she had purchased earlier that week. I sat in my chair watching her. *I hate having to rely on people. I used to make my own bed.* "Okay, I need to go. "You get some rest," she said kissing me on the cheek. "Thanks for helping," I said.

Later that afternoon we met some friends for dinner. It was a restaurant I especially liked. I fantasized about eating there again; a fluffy baked potato and a succulent piece of char broiled chicken. My mouth watered thinking about it. *I'm going to savor every bite.* I was ecstatic to be going. Our friends drove us to the restaurant early to avoid the crowds. Steven pushed my wheelchair up the sloping ramp following the waitress. I could hear him muttering under his breath about how hard it was.

"Pull me up to the table. I'll transfer into the booth," I said.

"Are you sure?" he said.

"Yes, yes, I'm sure. Don't treat me like I'm severely disabled, I want to feel normal," I said annoyed.

He helped me transfer, then folded my chair and placed it in the corner. The waitress handed us menus and took our drink order. "I'll be back," she said smiling. When she returned, she started writing down the orders. It was a challenge for me to order my meal. I couldn't stop laughing to tell her what I wanted. *This is awful! What am I even laughing about? I must be nervous!* Steven informed the waitress what happened explaining that it was the first time I had been out for a meal with some real food. *She's going to think I've been locked up for months. I hate having to explain what happened.*

The waitress smiled, "It's okay, Kate, take your time."

The meal was marvelous, and I was grateful to be able to swallow each bite.

"I bet that tastes great after all the hospital food, Kate," Rhonda said.

"No kidding, hospital food is very tasteless," I replied. "I need to be cautious drinking my water, to take only small sips," I said lifting the glass to my lips. *Lord knows I don't need a coughing episode in here. I also don't really want to have to use the bathroom. I'm not comfortable about that. Gone are the days when I could run into a bathroom.* I dreaded having to use a bathroom in a public place, especially with the wheelchair. Now I really appreciated the handicap stalls in bathrooms.

We went to church that evening and I insisted that we enter while the service was in session.

"I don't want people running up to me," I told Steven. As we proceeded into the room, a few heads turned around but the majority of the congregation watched the pastor giving his sermon. Steven quietly pushed the wheelchair along the back of the room where we sat listening to the Pastor. Glancing up from his reading, he noticed us sitting there, paused for a moment and took his glasses off, "I think we have a member who has something important to say." Heads turned as he walked down the aisle holding a microphone. *No Zac, please don't walk down here. I hope you aren't walking this way! I just want to sit here. I'm not ready for this! Please don't make me say something.*

Before I knew it, he was kneeling beside me. "Welcome back Kate, do you have anything you want to say?" he asked. *Anything I want to say? I just wish you hadn't put me on the spot here.* Suddenly, I started crying uncontrollably. *What's happening? I had intended to speak, but I can't get any words out.*

"It's okay, Kate, I'm sorry if I overwhelmed you," he said touching me on the shoulder. The congregation rose to their feet applauding me. "We are all so proud of you," he said. I sat sobbing in my chair. *Now I really feel embarrassed! I wish they would stop clapping.* When the applause died down the Pastor went back to giving his sermon. *Why did I have to cry like that? I felt stupid.* After the service, the congregation members came over to greet me. *This feels overwhelming. Living outside of the hospital is going to be much worse than I ever imagined!*

On a daily basis nurses came to my house to assist me in getting showered and dressed. *There must be a way to do this myself. This is an adjustment; I hate having to rely on people. I feel like a broken doll that can't be fixed.* I could wheel my chair up to the edge of the shower door but I needed help closing it. Everything seemed overwhelming.

Seeing the disarray in my house made me angry, depressed and frustrated. *How could Steven have allowed this to happen? I want to get up out of this wheelchair and fix everything. I feel helpless.* I was frustrated with myself and disappointed with all the people around me.

I was especially disappointed with the home care I was receiving. The therapists who came to my house to give me OT and PT were well meaning but it was nothing like I had become accustomed to receiving at Daniel Freeman. *If I continue with this, I'll never leave my wheelchair behind.* I complained to Steven and expressed my concern.

In my next outpatient evaluation session that Steven and I attended we were asked what I wanted to achieve. I told the therapists I wanted to be independent and walk again. Steven made clear his unhappiness about the home therapy. He asked the case manager for some suggestions, and she told him they had a wonderful outpatient program, but my insurance company would not cover it.

Steven would once again have to go toe to toe with the insurance company. Putting some kind of argument together, Steven got the company to agree to pay the outpatient therapy only if I agreed to waive home nursing help. It was complicated but it worked out for me.

Even though Steven was doing so much, I found myself each day feeling more and more anger toward him. I could not get over how badly he had managed the house and the nanny.

Thanks to the deal Steven worked out, I was able to continue outpatient therapy at Daniel Freeman. Therapy was going to be five days a week. I remember one of my therapists asking me my goals that first day. "What kinds of goals do you have in outpatient therapy, Kate?" Herlene asked.

"I just want to get the use of my arm back. You have to help," I said with a sense of urgency.

"That is a goal of ours too, but is there anything you want to accomplish while you are here?" she asked.

I'm going to express my desire to her. If only I could hold my daughters. "I want to be able to lift my daughters up," I told her.

"Well, let's see how we can attain that," she said. *How am I going to do that?*

During the weekly therapy sessions Herlene practiced with me by improvising with two round balls placed into a pillowcase.

"Okay, Kate, let's pretend this is your daughter and you are going to pick her up," Herlene said. I started laughing. *Right!* "No laughing, Kate, you have to concentrate," she said.

"But this seems so silly," I told her.

"Well you do want to hold your daughters again, don't you?" Herlene asked. *Yes, you are right. I'm willing to try anything.* At first I struggled with one hand to grasp the balls trying to imagine I was holding Rachel.

At home I practiced with the girls asking them to stand on the couch so I could lift them. The nanny stood by ready to catch them.

"Look nanny. Mom is holding me," Stephanie said. *Don't wriggle around too much Stephanie. I need to stay steady. I'm nervous holding you.* "Good job mom," Stephanie said.

"Okay girls, Mum has to rest," I told them. *It feels good reaching my goal of holding them.* (Gradually over the months I was able to comfortably hold them close, although I could not walk around with them. I had to stand in one spot. The girls loved taking turns being held.)

Thursday of that week I had therapy and Steven insisted on going with me. *I really wish he wouldn't come today. I am not in a great mood.*

"I have an appointment with a new social worker," I told him.

"Oh good, I'd like to be there and meet her," he said. He drove me to the hospital where I met the social worker first. Wheeling me to her office, he knocked on the door. We were greeted with a warm smile.

"Hi, I'm Susan Hopper, please come in. You must be Kate. It's nice to meet you." After Steven introduced himself, she motioned him to a chair. I stayed in the wheelchair. "I've read over your file, and it's quite a story," she said.

"How is it being home?" she asked. "It's still a challenge, but I believe we'll get through it," *Steven* responded. My mind wandered as they spoke. *This is a waste of time. I hate having to go through this! I'd rather have therapy and work on my arm. I wish I still had Amy as my social worker; I don't want a new one. I feel on edge today.* I had many feelings bottled up inside me.

"How are you feeling since you returned home Kate?" Susan asked me.

"My house is in a shambles," I said frustrated. Turning I looked at Steven. "You should have seen things were in order. How could you do that?" I asked aggravated.

"I'm sure he did the best he could under the circumstances," the social worker said.

"I did everything I could, Kate. I felt that saving your life was more important than taking care of the house," he expressed. We argued back and forth. Steven went on to explain, "We have a nanny who had been our daughter's pre-school teacher. She quit her job to come and take care of our kids. She seemed so stable, but I was to learn very shortly that the task of caring for the children in this emergency has been too much for her. I'm looking into getting her replaced."

I'm still disappointed in you for allowing the house to come to this condition. I'm home and I can't let this upset me. I wish I hadn't come here at all. Trying to control myself, I felt the feelings surface. Tears started to roll down my cheeks. *I knew this would happen. That's exactly why I didn't want him to come today. I have therapy soon. How am I supposed to concentrate?*

The session turned into a nightmare with me crying uncontrollably. I couldn't even speak because I was so upset. I listened to him ramble on about his health issues and Susan nodded in agreement.

This is supposed to be a therapy session for me, not him! I'm the one who had the stroke! No one understands how I feel. How would they know what it's like? It wasn't fair. I was angry inside, mad with him, her, the world! *Life isn't fair! My world has been turned upside down!*

The hour went by quickly and Susan announced the session had ended. *This was a total waste of time. I feel worse.* "I'll see you next week Kate. I'm sorry this was upsetting for you."

Steven wheeled me down the hallway and I just sobbed into some tissue. My face was red and my eyes puffy. "How am I suppose to have therapy now?" I cried out waving my arm in the air. "You have upset me! Are you happy?" I asked. *I need to pull myself together; I've got to get through therapy. I can't let this happen again and interfere with my therapy. I have to concentrate. It's overwhelming enough to try to coordinate things at home and focus on therapy.*

I gave myself a pep talk. I had a session of therapy to get through. I just couldn't focus. Susan walked in during therapy.

"Kate, I can see you next Thursday after your therapy session," she said.

Oh no you won't! I have no intentions of coming next Thursday.

"Thank you Susan for rearranging, Kate's schedule," Steven said.

Therapy didn't go well and the therapist suggested I go home and rest. *I hate missing therapy. I just can't focus being this upset. Damn those two!*

There was silence between us on the drive home. A couple of times, Steven tried bringing up the subject.

"I can't talk about this. I don't want to talk about it," I said firmly. *I know I'm going to start crying if he brings this up again. I can feel myself getting upset.*

We arrived at the house and he wheeled me inside.

"How was therapy Kate?" Amanda asked. I started to cry again.

"It wasn't a good session," Steven replied.

I rolled down my ramp and into my room. I went to bed refusing to speak to anyone. *Today was not how I had planned. I'm depressed and have a raging headache.* I lay on my bed; my head spinning, wishing I hadn't let myself get that upset. *I don't care anymore but I've come so far. I can't give up now. Look how far I've come. I'm not going back to that social worker, to heck with them all! I just don't care about the house, therapy, anything! God, change my thinking.* I slept the remainder of the day.

—⁓⁓⁓—

The next day I called the women's Pastor and told her I wanted a divorce and that I also wanted to move back to New Zealand. She was stunned, but listened, asking if she could help.

The following day the doorbell rang, and I found myself confronted by the senior Pastor, his chief assistant and the women's pastor. *So much for trusting her!* They had come to help Steven and me "save our marriage." I felt like I was being placed on trial. Steven acted as if he had no idea this was coming. I told my story and Steven told his. The pastors asked questions and then came the verdict.

"Kate, it sounds like you are making a molehill into a mountain. We understand how you feel, but Steven has been a good man," Pastor Zac said.

Making a molehill into a mountain? How do you people know what I'm going through? The church, which had been so important to me suddenly seemed like they were against me in a war between Steven and me.

Steven had failed to take care of my precious house or manage the nanny, and his habits drove me nuts. I always knew he was a slob, but now I could not do anything to fix it. I did not mind when I was healthy walking behind him cleaning up the path of destruction he left in his wake. I made my mind up that I wanted a divorce. I wanted to take the kids and go back to New Zealand.

The following Thursday I was supposed to meet Susan, but I canceled.

"Kate, I won't come with you this time," Steven said.

"No, I'm not going. I don't like her as much as Amy," I said. I stayed in bed canceling physical therapy as well.

That night, sensing something was wrong, Steven insisted I go out to dinner with him. During dinner I told him that I wanted a divorce. He said no, but I told him I was unhappy.

"I deserve to be happy especially after my ordeal. I feel I deserve to be happy. I've paid such a high price to stay alive and I'm entitled to be happy. You are annoying, pushy and a slob." I said.

Steven replied, "Kate, you are not unhappy because of me but because of the stroke. I will not help you in any way if you wish to proceed with a divorce." He gave me a lecture on the sacredness of marriage. *I don't want to hear that, what I want is to be away from you!* The dinner produced a truce but I was very attached to the idea of getting away from this man.

Susan called during the next morning and I chatted briefly with her. We decided I would go to the appointment next week without Steven. I could agree to that. *After all, the sessions are for my benefit. I'm the one who has had this traumatic event in life.* Over the months I began to trust Susan, and I expressed myself. I looked forward to my sessions, finding her compassionate and caring. *I'm glad now I decided to stay with her. I like her.*

I tried to work out my feelings about Steven, but I was still very unhappy with our relationship.

—∿— —∿— —∿—

Sitting at my kitchen table one afternoon, I heard the doorbell ring. *I wonder who that is? It's like Grand Central Station here.* I wheeled toward the front door.

"Just a minute," I called. I pushed myself up the ramp, rolling onto the tile floor. Opening the door, I saw a woman in her late 40s standing there. She looked athletic, wearing a T-shirt, bicycling shorts and biking shoes. Leaning against the wall was her bike. *I hope she's not selling something. She must be at the wrong house. I don't know this person.*

"Kate? You don't know me, but I'm Mary. I'm from the church, and have been praying for you. May I come in?" she said. I wheeled myself down my ramp. She followed me into the kitchen. Wheeling my chair by the table, Mary pulled a chair out for herself.

"You do very well with the wheelchair," she said sitting down.

"Well, I've had lots of practice," I replied.

"Kate, I wanted to come by sooner. Actually, I asked the pastor to drop this off, but he felt I should come by myself," she said handing me something. It was a gold medal attached to a long blue ribbon. *A medal?*

Mary continued. "I felt bad when I heard what had happened to you, and I knew you were an athlete. I used to see you working out at the gym. I prayed and God told me to run a triathlon in your honor. During the race I just kept praying, Kate, you've got to make it! You have to do this! Fight Kate! I kept telling myself, I'm going to win this for Kate."

I sat speechless listening to her. Mary proceeded, "I told myself, you have to win this race. I wanted to quit, my legs were tired and my feet were aching. But I knew I had to cross that finish line. Halfway through the race, a man was running neck to neck with me. I told him why I was running and that I had to win this race. He said I deserved to win and not to give up. He let me get out in front. I told myself, I'm going to win and I'm going to cross that line. Tears were rolling down my cheeks and I just sobbed and sobbed as I crossed the finish line. I did this for you Kate. You have been my inspiration and I thought if you can fight to get your life back, then I can win this race."

Mary sat back in the chair taking a deep breath.

Wow. This is amazing! I sat there clutching the medal. A chill ran down my spine. "This means a lot to me and I want to thank you. I'm a little overwhelmed right now and don't know what to say," I said.

Patting me on the hand she said, "Well, I finally got up the courage to bring it by. I'm glad you are finally home and onto the road to recovery." As she spoke, I was reminded of the verse in 2nd Timothy: *I have fought the good fight, I have finished the race, and I have kept the faith.*

"Thank you, Mary, thank you," I said seeing her to the door.

"Bye, Kate, I'll be praying for you," Mary said giving me a warm hug. *My story has touched a lot of people. I can make a difference. I wish I hadn't gone through all this suffering. Thank you God for giving me a second chance.*

CHAPTER SIXTEEN

Back in the Driver's Seat

Being home from the hospital was wonderful, but I was faced with many challenges that could not have been anticipated. My children and husband had been like a breath of fresh air, and I was overjoyed to be home with them. Unfortunately, my jubilation did not last long as time went on and I began to resent all of the work needed to raise two small children and take care of the needs of my husband, Steven. *I still have to start my life all over again, yet how am I expected to take care of everyone? I can't even drive myself to therapy. I need some independence!*

The turning point in my recovery came when I could drive again. It had been six months since my stroke and I wasn't seeing any progress. Feeling depressed, I needed a milestone and expressed my desire to drive again to my therapist. "I need to drive again," I told her. "I'm tired of relying on other people. I can't wait to have some independence of my own."

"Okay, Kate, we'll test you on Monday. Diane Chavez will be testing you," Susie said. *Really? I'm nervous already.* Daniel Freeman had their own driving evaluation that meets DMV standards.

I practiced driving with Steven that weekend, leaving the girls with the nanny, so I could concentrate. We went to a large parking lot and I got into the drivers seat. *Wow! This feels great!* It felt very natural even though the left side of my body was paralyzed. (Of course, if the car had been a stick shift I could not have managed.) I drove confidently around and instead of letting

Steven take the wheel, I kept on driving out of the lot and all the way home. *Yes! I'm ready to be driving again.*

"Good job, Kate, I think you will have no problem. Now you'll be able to drive yourself to therapy," he said. I remember being nervous Monday morning when I came to therapy. My two hours of therapy were spent evaluating my progress.

"Ready?" Diane asked coming to get me. "Yes I'm ready to get behind the wheel," I said enthusiastically. "First I need to go over a few basic rules before we do the actual road test," she said.

Rules? I know how to drive and I know the rules on the road. I followed her in my wheelchair and we went into a small room.

"Okay I need to do a series of tests and I'll be timing you," Diane said.

Tests? She saw my look of apprehension, "Don't worry, Kate, you'll do fine. These just tell me how quick your response is."

Diane had a sequence of tests involving cognitive testing, visual perception and reaction time. She had me cover one eye while reading the alphabet for her. A machine with traffic lights on it tested my reaction time as the lights moved from green to amber and then red.

"How am I doing?" I asked.

"Fine, okay, we have one more test to do," she said. The test was to see how my eyes reacted to light for night driving. She turned off the lights in the room. "Kate, some lights will appear shining toward you for five seconds. You have one to three seconds to react," she said.

Okay, I'm ready. She ran her test.

"Good, Kate, I think we can do the road test now," she said turning the lights on. *I feel relieved that part is over.*

The final hour involved the actual road test. Diane wheeled my chair to the street level where the car was.

"How am I going to manage putting the wheelchair in my car?" I asked her.

"Someone will help you, but you are learning to use a walker, right?" she said.

"Yes," I said. I transferred from the wheelchair to the driver's seat. Diane explained everything while in the car.

"This is a dual-equipped car, so any time you feel nervous, I can take over," she said.

"What is this funny looking thing?" I asked.

"That is called a steering wheel knob to help you turn corners," Diane explained.

"I'm going to need one of those?" I asked.

"Believe me. You'll love it. It will come in handy. You're probably too young to remember but years ago truckers had them. They were called necking knobs but now they are illegal unless you have a physical need," she said. *Well, I don't plan to be necking with anyone!*

I glanced around the car and adjusted the mirrors. Reaching with my good hand, I clicked the seat belt in place. *This will take some getting use to with one hand.* As I turned the key I saw a long, thin piece of metal sticking out from the side of the wheel. "And this?" I asked.

"That's a turn signal when you want to change lanes," she said. *That's good. Somebody thought of everything.*

Cautiously I drove the surface streets to my house. "I'd like to stop by and see the girls and grab my sunglasses if you don't mind," I asked her.

"You are behind the wheel," Diane answered laughing. We stopped by my house briefly and the girls were surprised to see me.

"Mom, what are you doing here?" Stephanie asked puzzled.

"Your mom is learning to drive," Diane told her.

"Please let me come, please," Stephanie pleaded.

"No, I need to concentrate, but soon honey," I told her. The nanny helped to get the girls and we left. Diane suggested we take the freeway back to the hospital. *Take the freeway?*

"Are you sure I'm ready for that?" I asked.

"There's only one way to find out. I wouldn't suggest it if I didn't feel comfortable," she said. I did fine driving on the free-way feeling confident using the steering wheel knob; it helped with turning corners. We pulled up at the hospital and I parked the car.

"Well, Kate, you did great and have passed the driving evaluation," she said.

"That's it?" I asked her.

"The only apparatus you'll need is a steering wheel knob and a turn signal, but otherwise you are ready," she said. *This is great! I needed this milestone.* "I have to give the information to Dr. Alexander and he has the final say. I strongly recommend you don't drive until you get the equipment," she advised. *I can't wait to drive. I want to do it now.*

Steven drove my car the next day and had the apparatus put on.

"I want to drive myself to therapy. I'll take your car," I told him.

"Are you sure?" he asked. "Yes, I know I'll be fine and I'll take the surface streets," I reassured him.

"What about the wheelchair?" he asked.

"I'll use my walker this morning. I have to practice anyway," I said. The sense of freedom felt wonderful. I was on cloud nine. I turned the volume up on the radio, singing cheerfully to the music. *This feels great! I feel normal again.*

I was in therapy when Diane walked up to me.

"Hi, Kate, how did you get to therapy this morning? Did someone drive you?" she asked. *Why is she asking me that? Did she see me?*

"Yes, I got here okay," I slowly responded.

"You didn't know that was me in front of you this morning, did you?" she said laughing.

"You were?" I said shocked. *Oh my! She did see me driving.*

Diane grinned, "Yes, you couldn't wait to drive, even without your equipment on the car?" *Okay, so she caught me. I can't believe she was in front of me.*

"My husband took the car I'll be driving to have the equipment put on and I just wanted to drive so badly," I told her. "Well, you looked like you were doing fine. I was watching you," Diane said. All of us laughed and I went back to concentrating on therapy.

Of course, one of my first driving outings was to the mall. I remember driving up to the valet. "Hi, would you mind helping me?" I pulled the latch for the trunk. "I need help getting my wheelchair out of my trunk," I said. The valet assembled my chair and I proudly wheeled myself into the entrance of the mall. *This feels great! I can go shopping on my own. After all, a girl's got to shop.*

The goal to drive again after a stroke was an important one. It was not merely a luxury to drive again, but a necessity. Many survivors, who at one time drove for years, suddenly become filled with fear at the thought of learning again. *Can I do this? What if I don't succeed? I don't know if I should even bother trying.* Many don't sleep the night before their driving lesson and are filled with apprehension. It's a wonderful transformation to see the changed attitude of a survivor who can drive again. Charlie Corn, who works with survivors to get them behind the wheel again, tells it like it is.

"Anyone can drive," he says. "They have to compensate for their problems. With the right adaptive equipment they can be driving again. It's important to have training so the patient is safe driving."

Every DMV office has a driver's safety program. This is for anyone who has had a medical problem. Some applicants, who have been driving for 30 years prior to their stroke, assume they will have no trouble passing the test. The regulatory test runs 25 minutes, and the driver safety officer has been told how to test the applicant. Things that are covered in the test are: vision perception, reaction time, functional ability and the actual on-the-road test. Sometimes the applicant has a lengthy waiting period for the results. In order to feel comfortable and confident with the adaptive equipment, training is necessary. Today with more drivers on the road, raised speed limits and large trucks, it's important to have driver safety programs available.

Now that I was home, I started to take an interest in my appearance again. The first thing I worked on was the hideous brace. I decided that I would have it cut down. I had discussed it with my therapist who told me to see Michael Jefferies. I drove to his office.

"Are you sure you want me to do that?" he asked.

"Yes, I'm positive, the brace won't look so noticeable," I said. *I hope I'm doing the right thing, I know my appearance will look better.* "That's true but you won't have the knee control," Michael replied. "Oh please, I know the knee control will be fine," I said. The brace was cut so it sat midway at my calf.

(Several years after my stroke, I had a new brace made, realizing the benefit of having the brace up to my knee. The brace keeps my knee from snapping back. I also realized that by wearing long pants no one could see my brace under them. It has taken this long for me to feel comfortable enough to wear this brace and not be concerned what people think.)

As I look back now, I can laugh at myself. I remember one day going into outpatient rehab with a beautiful pair of shoes, trying to convince my therapist that I could wear them. Sitting in my wheelchair, I held up the shoes.

"Look Herlene, aren't these beautiful?" I took off my tennis shoes and struggled to put on the shoes that were made out of animal skin. I squeezed my brace into the left shoe adjusting the straps. *I'm exhausted but at least I have them on.* The shoes were all heel and straps.

"I could have the heel cut down," I said.

"They certainly are beautiful, but I don't think they are

appropriate," Herlene said. *I know she knows deep down that I know these aren't appropriate.*

"But doesn't my right foot look sexy in these?" I asked.

Herlene laughed, "Kate, the only way you could wear those shoes is if you gave up walking and remained in the wheelchair." *But they look so beautiful on my feet and they weren't cheap! I guess she is right. The shoes will have to go back or I could wear them if people would wheel me around. I could hide my brace.*

The shoes were returned to the store and replaced with a simple style. *I've always been a shoe hog; I hate to return these.* When you suddenly go from cute shoes to flat, basic, matronly Velcro-ones, this is a major challenge. More so, finding a pair of shoes that is attractive yet functional with a brace is not an easy task. Heels are History! That was the end of me assuming I could wear those kinds of shoes. Like the saying goes; If the shoe doesn't fit, don't force it.

Even today I longingly look at other women's shoes and wish I could wear them. Then I remember what I've been through and realize that wearing any kind of shoe is a miracle for me. When I have that desire to wear those shoes, it takes me back to the time that shoes weren't the issue but taking my next breath was. That seems to put shoes and life in perspective.

Feeling ready to talk with others about my stroke, one evening my friend Jenny agreed to drive me to a stroke support meeting in West L.A. I had attended a couple of other groups but found I couldn't relate. I was so much younger than the others and had two small children. My issues were different from those of a senior. I felt uncomfortable in the beginning with this group, which was for stroke survivors 55 and under but decided to join anyway. I soon warmed up to the group. It was there that I met another courageous stroke survivor named Candace. One meeting, I asked Candace how she started her group, "Different

Strokes for Different Folks." She encouraged me to start my own group in my area and referred me to the Stroke Association's executive director, Susan Blatt, for guidance. I really wanted to help others like myself and I was excited to start a group. Susan told me to first look for a location and get back to her.

Calling a couple of hospitals to see about starting a group, one woman asked me, "What are your credentials?" *Credentials? No one knows more about a stroke than me; I've been through it*

"I've had a stroke!" I replied. The woman explained that someone from administration would get back to me. I proved that old saying true; "You have to get a lot of no's to get one yes." Instead of hearing no, I heard, try again. I was determined to start a group. I then met with an administrator from Beach Cities Hospital and convinced her there was a need for a stroke support group. We talked over details and the "Back on Track" group was founded. Starting the group gave me back my sense of independence and self-esteem. I had flyers made up and posted them all over my community. The word spread and soon the "Back on Track" group grew. By reaching out and helping others, I was helping myself in my recovery.

The executive director of the Stroke Association was pleased that a new support group had started and asked if I would like to help out by raising funds for the health fair. The Stroke Association here in California was having their annual health fair with a 5K walk/run. I was honored, and again, it gave me the chance to have something else to focus on. I had suggested to Susan that since I had small children it would be great to have one of those huge blow-up bouncers for kids.

"Well, we really don't have many kids at the event," Susan replied.

"Well, young people have strokes and I'm sure a lot of these people coming must have kids and grandchildren," I said.

"That's something I'll bring up to the board, but I'd love you to sell some raffles tickets and maybe get together a team," Susan

Kate's "Back on Track" stroke support group

said. I ended the phone call telling her I'd come by her office that next morning.

Susan handed me a stack of raffle tickets to sell on their behalf. I came home and started organizing my team of walkers and selling the raffle tickets. I was excited to raise money for the organization and decided I would hold a bake sale at my house and have my own kid's bouncer in the backyard. I had many friends with small children and knew it would be a great little fund-raiser. Friends would bake different things, and I'd have flyers made for the big day.

I was still in outpatient therapy and that week I focused on my cooking ability to make banana bread. Mum had given me a wonderful no-fail recipe for banana bread years ago, and it was about the only cake I could bake well.

In outpatient therapy there was a small kitchen off to the side where patients learned to cook again. Not only did I do a lot of reaching in the cupboards for ingredients but I also had to concentrate on the rest of my body. My therapist was at my side while I stood trying to bear weight on my left leg, squeezing my butt and stomach tight while keeping my shoulder blades squeezed. I had to watch that my left arm wasn't hanging limp. It was difficult to stir the mixture with my one good arm and think of all these things at the same time. While the cake was baking, I cleaned up my mess (at the request of my therapist) leaving a spotless kitchen for the next patient. Just doing that simple task was more therapy. Before long the aroma of the fresh bread baking could be smelt throughout the kitchen and therapy room. The therapists popped their heads in the kitchen to see if the bread was ready. *There has to be a way I can raise money here. That's what I'll do. I'll sell slices of bread to raise money!*

Mum's Famous Banana Bread

> 1 Egg
> 1 cup sugar
> 1¾ cup flour
> 1 teaspoon baking powder
> 4 ozs butter
> 2 mashed bananas (the older the better!)
> 1 teaspoon baking soda dissolved in ½ c milk (added last)

Cream butter and sugar until light and fluffy, add egg and beat. Using a wooden spoon, gradually fold in flour, baking powder and mashed bananas: then add soda and milk. Bake in a loaf tin approx 50-60 minutes at 350°.
Good baking!

That week I baked banana bread, selling warm slices to the therapists for $1 each. I held my fund-raiser on a Saturday and many friends stopped by. The kids loved jumping in the bouncer and their parents donated money for the Stroke Association.

Monday morning I took $1,000 in cash into the Stroke Association. Susan was thrilled. "This is wonderful, Kate, I would love to clone about 10 of you," she said. Before the big health fair Susan asked me if I'd like to be a director on the board and I could meet many of the board members at the event. I was extremely happy. The day of the event, I wore a ribbon that hung with the word "director" on it. It was a great morning with many walkers and runners out raising money for the cause. I focused on other people and how I could help them. Becoming a director with the Stroke Association gave me that opportunity while I still worked in therapy. *I'm feeling like I'm back in the driver's seat!*

Another fund-raising project I helped to coordinate was a fashion show with Nordstroms as the sponsor. I had been a frequent shopper there before my stroke and knew many of the salespeople. While raising money for the health fair, I had asked them to sponsor me. Someone suggested that I submit my story on behalf of the Stroke Association. So I did and waited anxiously for their response. I approached the Stroke Association at a board meeting and told them of my idea. They gave me their blessings with a moderate amount of enthusiasm.

I worked closely with Nordstroms and attended several fashion shows to see how they were organized. I prepared more than 400 names of my own for my list of invitees. Each director had to hand in their list of 20 names to the Association. We were scheduled for an April fashion show, and Nordstroms did an outstanding job of securing the models and offering an unbelievable show. As the guests arrived, they were greeted and given a light buffet breakfast. The stage was in place and the runway show was amazing with beautiful models showing the latest spring fashions. The fashion show was a success. Money was raised and the event helped to raise awareness of strokes and stroke prevention. These two events were the start of my fund-raising for the Stroke Association. I became very active as a director on the board attending numerous health fairs on behalf of the organization.

My story was going to be featured in an upcoming issue of *Stroke Connection*, a national magazine published by the American

Heart Association. The Heart Association held their annual International Joint Conference on Stroke in California, February 1996. I received a call one day from Elizabeth, a staff member from the magazine, who was working on the article asking me if I could possibly come down to Anaheim and briefly speak.

"Kate this would be great if you could speak, that way everyone will be able to put a name to the face when the article comes out," Elizabeth told me.

"Okay, I'll do it," I said. *I haven't spoken before except to a few stroke groups. I hope it's not a lot of people.*

Arriving at the conference I met Elizabeth who hurried me into the room where the luncheon was taking place. I gasped at the number of people sitting at tables.

"Here, Kate, let's sit you here. This is Barbara Jackson," she said introducing me to each person at the table. *I'm going to speak before this many people?*

"How many people are in this room Barbara?" I asked.

"Oh this is an annual International Stroke Conference of 1800 and this year we are meeting here. A lot of these people are neurologists, surgeons, physicians and nurses in the field of strokes," she said.

"And I'm going to speak before them?" I said.

"Don't worry, you'll do fine. They will love you and before they leave today you'll be a household name," she said laughing.

Barbara helped me onto the stage. I stood behind the podium feeling my legs shaking, my heart pounding. *You can do this. Just stay calm.* As I spoke, you could have heard a pin drop. I mentioned the *Stroke Connection* magazine as Barbara had instructed. I started feeling at ease standing up there. The 10 minutes went by quickly and the crowd broke into applause as I left the stage. *Wow! I really enjoyed that.* As I sat down at my table, I realized that I could make a difference in other people's lives. *I can help someone else who is hurting.*

"Great job, Kate, that was wonderful. Kirk Douglas couldn't have done a better job," Barbara said.

"Kirk Douglas?" I asked.

"Yes we were trying to get him to speak but he wasn't available," she said. *How exciting! I'm getting to fill in for Kirk Douglas.*

I went onto to become a national volunteer spokesperson for the American Heart Association. (AHA) I became involved speaking locally at stroke support groups and furthered my speaking interest by joining my local chapter of the National Speakers Association. There I met others in the speaking business, and it wasn't long before I was being paid for speaking. I decided to become a board member with my local AHA division, involving my kids in events to raise funds.

In November of 1997, a new nationwide division solely for stroke survivors was named the American Stroke Association. (ASA) I have spoken at various affiliates throughout the country. As a volunteer spokesperson, I was asked to testify before the United States Congress, to gain more funds for stroke and heart research. (My speech is reprinted in the appendix.)

I remember that trip to Washington and how I felt in the courtroom. The chamber was packed with reporters and television cameras. There were bright lights and you could hear the clicking of cameras. Disabled people sat in their wheelchairs. There wasn't a seat left in the room. My husband wheeled me in, maneuvering the chair into a corner. *Why is it so busy in here?*

"That's Muhammad Ali sitting there," he whispered. *The real Muhammad Ali? Why is he here?* I listened closely as I heard his wife testifying for him on behalf of the Parkinson's Disease society. After her speech, she escorted her husband out with reporters and cameramen following him. *I'm glad I don't have that kind of audience listening to me as I talk.*

When it was my turn to speak and I was sitting at the table I read the words in front of me. I had exactly five minutes to speak before one of the congressmen hit a gong letting me know my time was up. My speech had been carefully looked over by the AHA people and changed a little before the final copy was given to me to read. I was familiar with most of it, but I read with my head down occasionally looking up. It was a nervous experience to be speaking before Congress. *These people are human just like me. There's nothing to be scared of.* I was relieved when it was over. *Thank goodness I got through that.*

In 1997, I gave another speech in Washington at the national mall in front of the Capitol. This was a live press conference where I shared the podium with Senator Barbara Boxer and Representatives Maxine Waters and Connie Morrel. Other speakers came along with me to help launch the AHA campaign, *Take Wellness to Heart.* Behind the stage in the shape of the AHA logo were thousands of red and white carnations signifying women who do not survive strokes each year. The floral tribute covered the size of a football field with cranes available to allow aerial photos of the flowers. It served as a memorial to the half a million women who die of cardiovascular disease each year. More women die of strokes than breast cancer.

It was windy that morning and as I watched the other speakers at the podium, it suddenly dawned on me, *they have two hands to hold their notes. I need to let someone from the AHA know, otherwise I'm going to be left speechless as the notes fly through the air.* An AHA staff person devised a folder that I could tuck the page in as I read. This speech wasn't off the cuff and I had certain points that had to be covered. I was proud to be a part of this important campaign to help reach other women.

I started becoming comfortable with my disability and realized that I may never regain the use of my arm. Accepting my disability over the years has been the hardest thing.

We had found a wonderful Christian nanny to replace Amanda. I find that usually children are not afraid to ask direct questions. I remember when Stephanie was in the first grade and her teacher gave the children an assignment to write what was special about their parents and to draw a picture. Stephanie asked her daddy to help her put something together. It said:

Stephanie's mom is special because she did not die from her stroke. My little sister thinks mom had a stroke because she ate too much candy. I help mom walk and rest her dead arm on my shoulder.

She drew a picture of me with one arm missing.

Once a week I helped out in Stephanie's classroom. The teacher never gave me anything I couldn't handle; usually I helped with reading and observing the kids coloring. I remember after Stephanie had her show and tell, that following week I came to class like usual. When I walked into the room, all the kids ran up to me. *Wow! This is a greeting.* The intrigued children were eager to see my dead arm that Stephanie had told them about. Children are certainly very direct with their questions. Stephanie's friends often will ask, "What happened to your leg?" "Oh my mom had a stroke," Stephanie tells them casually. "What's a stroke?" they ask. "It means her arm and leg doesn't work properly," Stephanie replies. The children looked at me in bewilderment. Kids will be kids!

—⁓——⁓——⁓—

As the weeks turned into months, and with continued pressure on me, I found myself returning to some regular twelve-step support meetings that I had attended in the past. The kids were doing well. My pressure now came from being overwhelmed with my new life and unhappy with my marriage. It was at the meetings that I met a man who appeared to have all I wanted, a single man, without kids, who wanted me for me, where I could be myself without a care in the world. My marriage was in trouble, and I resented the family needing me to be there for them. *I was almost dead not long ago, and here I was expected to take care of them all the time! I have been through so much, and I wanted to live. I want to responsible for no one and nothing.* I was so lost and so overwhelmed. I was not thinking clearly at all when I decided to file for a divorce in November of 1998.

Steven and Kate

CHAPTER SEVENTEEN

Lessons Learned

Looking back, separating from Steven was an ugly mistake. Having said that, it's through our mistakes that we learn. Over the past few years, I have learned many lessons. On a daily basis, while I was gone, I yearned to be a full time mum with my daughters, knowing I was missing out on important years.

The stroke was not just a physical event, it was also an emotional and spiritual blow. However, hindsight is 20.20, while responses to 'trauma' in the moment can never be predicted. First the stroke hit me physically. I didn't know how to adjust to a body that functioned differently. I now had limitations to deal with. In addition I had the emotional and spiritual issues that arose. I lost a complete sense of who I was. I didn't know how to be 'Kate.'

My marriage was wrecked and I could see no way to save it. I felt it would take a new miracle—maybe a greater one—to restore the marriage, than the one that had restored my health and mobility.

When my divorce case was going through the system, I learned we could have the status of the marriage dissolved, yet leave the other issues to be finished later. That is what we did. At first, the girls visited me in my new home. Weekend visits went by quickly before their dad picked them up. It was nice where I was living, yet so far from everything. This town San Pedro, Point Ferman was less exciting than Cleveland in winter!

Tension between my daughters and me grew because of my new relationship. It was difficult for them to accept me being with anyone other than their father. My new beau was a man who sadly took great advantage of me. He saw how fragile I was and did everything he could to destroy my marriage. I paid dearly for my mistakes. I nearly lost my children. This new man had never had children and often lost his temper with my daughters. He made negative comments about their dad, which they took back home. This all caused tremendous tension for everyone.

"It would be fine if you didn't have kids," he'd tell me.

"Well I do, and I miss them very much. Besides, no matter what, Steven is their dad and he'll be around for a while," I repeatedly told him.

Finally, after a few months of arguing and trips in and out of court, Steven got full custody of the children with my rights limited to supervised visits.

On the last two occasions in court I had been representing myself, as I did not have the funds to keep hiring attorneys. The Superior Court of Los Angeles located downtown is a scary place if you aren't familiar with the legal system. Speaking in court was fine, except I did not know the legal system and I did not do well representing myself.

I was in the middle of a war, but in retrospect Steven never really went after me. I was not able to care for the girls full time and Steven only wanted to protect our daughters and get back with me. He refused to admit that a civil court could grant a divorce. He refused to recognize the divorce process and continually demanded we reconcile. I don't do well when someone demands I do something. Steven was trying to bring us together but he was pushing us farther and farther apart.

We had both exhausted our resources as a result of my stroke, and now the little we had left would be burned up on legal costs to wage a fight that no one wanted. Both of us are stubborn, which is one of the major reasons I am alive at the moment. But when it came to this fight, being stubborn only made things worse.

I did not know who to trust; everyone had a different story to tell. My girl friends for the most part supported me. I never stopped being grateful for all the love and support my family had given me when I was in the hospital, but somehow I linked my depression to them. I guess there is some truth in the old expression, "you only hurt the people you love."

Before this sorry episode was over, my family and I would lose all of what remained of our life together. We lost material items, which mattered very little when weighed against the harm done to our family emotionally, spiritually, and psychologically.

Now I began slowly to see the unfolding of another stupendous miracle that would see the restoration of marriage and my family. It has not been a short process. In fact, it has taken years to see even a small amount of progress.

Here I was estranged from the people I loved most, distrustful of the man who had fought so hard to save my life, depressed and irrational, adrift in the middle of a storm. I did not know how to drop anchor or how to restore what was lost. In fact I did not even want to restore the past. I felt that I had suffered so much, that I deserved something for myself. It is very common for people who have been through a serious illness to feel this way. I was so damaged emotionally that I felt like I had nothing to give to my children or to Steven. I constantly felt guilty about being inadequate and burdened by the demands of the whole world.

Steven refused to acknowledge that our divorce was valid. He kept insisting that he loved me and always would. He told me that for him marriage was eternal and that no matter what he would be my husband. I kept resenting his pushing himself on me. The more Steven insisted we should get back together the more I resisted. I was one mixed up girl! One of the best choices

I made was to seek outside help and start working through my feelings. I missed Steven and the girls dearly. I felt like a huge snowball rolling down a hill unable to stop.

It wasn't really necessary for Steven and me to be fighting; and after three law firms and huge legal expenses, I finally found a good divorce attorney, David Abrams. He agreed that Steven and I should work this out amicably, and was interested in the children's welfare. He set the foundation for re-establishing the relationship with my family and in the process became a good friend. David was skilled enough to navigate through the legal system making sure that everyone was protected. None of the attorneys in the past had done anything to help me at all. In a few short weeks Mr. Abrams did more than all of them. As a skilled mediator, he got both parties communicating with each other. This was such a blessing.

Right around Thanksgiving 2000 things began to change for Steven and me. Steven went through all kinds of trouble to find a last minute turkey. He found a local restaurant that was willing at an extra expense to make a full-blown turkey dinner. Here I was with my family, or was it my family again? It had been three years since all of us sat down and gave thanks together. Here I could see there was something very real, a tie that winds of circumstances could not change.

Earlier that week the new man presented me with an ultimatum; he was demanding that I choose him or my children. Now, I may have been out of my mind, but that crazy I could never be. I don't see how any mother could make that kind of choice. Talking with my therapist helped immensely. I knew what my choice would be.

Shortly after Christmas I gave up the house in San Pedro and moved into a small quest house in Manhattan Beach to be near Steven and the girls. It's not like things changed overnight, but I knew in my heart that the best thing for our family was to be a family. First we agreed to make our children the focus of our lives and to try to do whatever was best for them. You don't have to be a rocket scientist to know that what is best for children is to have a loving mother and father at home. Putting our resentments aside we struggled to remain focused on raising the girls. I never thought I would have a life again with my daughters.

Now my life feels complete, and I can be there for Stephanie and Rachel as their Mum. Having a mom and a dad again has made a huge impact on the girls. They are no longer shuffled back and forth between two arguing parents. It has made life much simpler. Today we can do things as a family. When all is said and done, it's the kids that get hurt during divorce. Making the children our priority has been the best decision Steven and I could have made. Today, we work together, trying to undo the trauma done to the children. I realized through this process that this is a man who truly does love me and was there for me when I needed him most. This to me is true love!

I love being a family again. I was able to let go of my anger and resentments and realized that Steven is not the monster I made him out to be. We all have our pluses and minuses. No, he isn't perfect, but who is? I'm certainly not. It's miraculous and rates with Cinderella, and we really are going to try to live happily ever after.

CHAPTER EIGHTEEN

Incorporating Exercise
for Health and Recovery

Although I diligently exercised prior to my stroke, I do not have the same desire to exercise now. In the past, I loved fitting any form of exercise into my schedule. Today, I strive to do some exercise on a daily basis. I can do therapy with the help of a therapist encouraging me but on my own, I struggle to do the exercises. I have also found that assisted therapy lasts for a limited time due to insurance policy limitations. We all don't have the luxury of hiring a personal fitness trainer, but do check into your local YMCA. Many of them offer a trainer to help you get started after your initial sign-up.

With insurance companies cutting off benefits, it leaves many families wondering, "What do we do now?" During my outpatient therapy sessions, I coordinated a workbook explaining each exercise. Taking a camera into therapy, I had a friend take snapshots of me working with my therapist. The therapist wrote a sentence or two about each exercise. This helped immensely when I had to work alone at home.

An ongoing comment I receive from people around the country is, "My doctor has told me I won't get any better." The myth that a patient won't recover beyond six months after their stroke, in my opinion, is just that, a myth. It is true that the sooner a patient can get into a rehabilitation program, the quicker the return of motor function. However, in my experience, I've seen stroke patients recover well beyond a year post-stroke. I believe attitude plays a major role.

I participated in a program offered for the first time to physical therapy students at the University of Southern California (USC) as a hands-on training program for them. Taking several survivors from my stroke group, we committed to an hour and a half one day a week, twelve-week program. This was a wonderful opportunity that was free, and it gave us a chance to work on particular goals. At the beginning of the semester, we were videotaped and again at the end to measure our progress. We were given weekly exercises to work on.

The exercises on the following pages are part of a guideline that I use as a maintenance program. Covey Lazouras, a third year therapy student at the time with USC, was working with me every Tuesday, and graciously took part in these photos. Thanks Covey! You were not only fun but I learned a few things too! (Of course he just happened to be twenty-six years old, tall, dark and handsome. Needless to say, I was motivated to show up every Tuesday!)

Remember, what works for one person, may not work for another. Every stroke causes different injuries. So check with your doctor before trying any of these. A person's make-up, such as whether they are positive or assertive prior to their stroke, makes a definite difference in recovery. For me, I have found Pilates combined with some bridging is very beneficial. I know my body and its limitations. Again, I strongly stress checking with your doctor before starting an exercise program. Here are several beginning exercises to try.

BRIDGE EXERCISE
This one I call the 'bed pan' exercise.

1. Lie on the floor, bed or mat with both knees bent up with your feet flat on the floor.
2. Your feet should be in a neutral position pointing forward.
3. As you lift up your buttocks, tighten your stomach and buttock muscles. Concentrate on keeping both hips evenly off the ground.

4. Hold for a count of ten and slowly bring your hips down. Remember that your upper back does not rise off the floor.
5. Try a set for 10 times, then repeat.

HIP-CONTROL EXERCISE:

1. Lie on your back with both legs bent up, your feet in a neutral position.
2. Controlling the knee, slowly let the knee out.
3. Gradually return the knee to a neutral position.
4. Try a set of 10.

SHOULDER RANGE MOTION, SUPERMAN POSITION

For this exercise, you can use a broom handle or a wooden dowel from your local hardware store. This exercise can be done lying on your bed with your head hanging over the edge.

1. Lie on your stomach with your feet shoulde–width apart.
2. Make sure your neck is in a neutral position, looking down.
3. Raise the bar up to your shoulders, hold, then gradually back down. Your hands should be shoulder width apart.
4. Repeat 10 times.

Another exercise with the bar is to raise it to your chin with both elbows bent. You may have to bring your hands in closer. Control the bar as you slowly bring it down. This stabilizes your scapula.)

Purchasing one of these exercise balls is a good investment. Your therapist can get it for you. The vinyl balls come in three different colors: green, orange and blue. Check with your therapist on the color for you.

BALANCING

Leaning over the ball, put your hands in position with your fingers spread evenly on the affected side. (This can be done without the ball.) Keep your elbows straight and your head in a neutral position. This exercise challenges all the muscles of the torso. It's a less threatening, weight bearing exercise on the joints. It enhances the muscles to work together through the hip and shoulder.

The use of stretchable latex-rubber bands for strength resistance is also extremely effective so check with your therapist for the appropriate resistance. The patient needs to be able to move through the range of motion 8 to 10 times.

For advanced exercises with the ball, make sure you have supervision.

WEIGHT BEARING

1. Leaning your torso over the ball, lift the strong arm.
2. Place all your weight on the affected arm. This is a good weight-bearing exercise.

AT THE GYM

Participating in some form of exercise on a daily basis improves us mentally and emotionally. I find my depression is less, and for me, being able to work out a little in a gym again makes me feel normal. This was such a big part of my life prior to my stroke. At my local gym, I try to do some muscle strengthening exercises for my lower extremities.

I use the stair-climbing machine for weight bearing on my weak leg. I try to bear weight on my left hand while holding on, however, sometimes it helps to strap my hand on. I can recall when I first started with this exercise. I could stair-climb for only five minutes. I slowly built up to twenty minutes on a low resistance. With the help of an assistant, I can ride a stationary bike for thirty minutes. The leg press machine is also very good but someone should stabilize your knee and ankle while the brace is off. (Recently, I have been able to do the leg press by myself on a lighter weight with more repetitions. I am able to stabilize my knee so it doesn't wobble and by concentrating on putting weight through the leg, I can do the exercise with my brace off. The weight is set at thirty-five pounds increasing to fifty-five pounds.)

—⚮— —⚮— —⚮—

With any exercise program, check with your doctor first and do what works for you. I no longer have the image that I have to build up a sweat to get a good work out. Since my stroke, I tire easily and, therefore, have to be careful not to overwork my body. Some days, I have more energy than other days. Remember to be patient with yourself and take it easy.

For Other Stroke Survivors

or those of you who have had a stroke, I have included some insights along the way that have helped me in my recovery. Unfortunately, there is no magical pill to bring people like us back to a fully functioning life. The biggest solution is a lot of hard work. The process is slow, and you don't see the immediate gains. One very important point to remember is that no two strokes are the same.

Many people contact me regarding a loved one who has had a stroke, asking for advice. I am not a medical professional and, therefore, am only offering my hope and encouragement. Every stroke patient reacts and recovers in a different way, so it's best not to compare. There is light at the end of the tunnel. Yet it truly is one day at a time, requiring a lot of patience.

Insurance concerns

Almost immediately the recovery process begins in ICU with some simple range of motion exercises. Once the patient enters a rehab program, the long road of recovery lies ahead of them. What has changed even since I was in hospital is the insurance company polices. Years ago a patient would have stayed in the hospital nine months recovering. Today a patient is lucky to get six weeks.

Each insurance policy has a criterion for rehabilitation. The government sets the criteria and a patient has to be able to perform a minimum of three hours of therapy in order to participate. The case manager needs to show that there is a team needed in order to make that recovery happen. The insurance companies are now making a decision whether or not a patient can enter a particular rehab. When you are dealing with an insurance company, it is best to find out if they have a case manager assigned to the case.

If a patient does not meet the criteria, the insurance company may put them into a skilled nursing program. Rehabilitation can be provided on several levels starting out in the acute phase in the hospital where a therapist comes to the room. The patient is then transferred to a rehab program where it could be at the skilled nursing level of approximately one hour of therapy a day. Acute rehabilitation is three hours of therapy a day, followed by a home health care program of several times a week. From there a patient goes into an outpatient program that is usually three times a week. A lot has changed with insurance companies and the responsibilities that case managers once had.

Although people are suspicious of the insurance case managers, many times they are the go-betweens for the adjuster and the medical team. It is a good idea to ask if there is a case manager involved because very often they will advocate for the patient even though the insurance company is paying them.

It is the insurance companies that make deals with hospitals. They pick the center of excellence bound by a contract. You have to go with those centers contracted with the insurance company; however if you are not happy with the facility you *do* have the choice to change. In my own case, I was making some change on a daily basis. My age had something to do with the decision.

Isa Anderson, director of case management at Daniel Freeman Hospital, receives calls from around the country. She offers this advice, "The patient needs an advocate who is willing to stand up for them. It's an overwhelming process, however there are things that can be done for the patient. The family member can sit down with a financial counselor at the hospital and review the patient's insurance policy. If they have difficulty in understanding the policy they can also review it with the insurance company membership advisor. Ask if there is an insurance case manager assigned to the patient. Find out who it is and ask questions. The advocate needs to be as educated as possible on the patient's policy. Speak with the patient's human resource department and inquire about the benefits the patient had with that employer. Its like that old saying, "the squeaky wheel gets the grease. Don't be afraid to speak up."

Health care advocate, Robert Donin, stresses, "Read the evidence of coverage even if you have to have someone read you the fine print." He also advises to know your doctor and have a good relationship so you can be prepared. Steven Klugman my renowned health care advocate says ask questions, ask questions, then ask questions again and make demands. He recommends you do as he did; always ask the doctors, "What would you do it that was your child?" Get someone to be your personal advocate, never try to do it alone. Never give up!

It's the squeaky wheel that gets the grease!

The work of rehabilitation and recovery

It is helpful for the family members to be assertive asking questions, especially if they are not seeing results in the patient's rehab recovery. Rehabilitation hospitals today encourage the family's involvement. A stroke survivor may not have the physical disability, yet they cannot express themselves. One man in my stroke group had trouble speaking and constantly had uncontrolled bursts of swearing and anger. Another survivor had no feeling on the affected side. Some cannot read or write. But what we have in common is the fact we have experienced a stroke. Knowing people who have gone down the same road and who are there to support them can alleviate a stroke survivor's fears. Having people listen as they speak reassures them to keep going.

In the frequent e-mails I receive from around the country, I'm asked what the survivor may be feeling. Depending upon what part of the brain has been affected, it will vary for each patient. Ask questions to the patient's doctor and find out what kinds of problems you can expect from their stroke. If you don't understand, ask the doctor to explain it in layman terms. Statistics show that the majority of recovery is in the first six months, yet from my own experience, my recovery continues on a daily basis. A patient has to be willing to put in the effort.

The key is that the patient must want to do the therapy. Too often I receive letters from a caregiver asking why they cannot motivate the survivor to do the therapy. The motivation has to come from the survivor. Nagging the survivor to do therapy will not help and will only diminish the recovery. When a doctor makes a statement to the family that there is no hope for a patient's recovery, they are merely going by statistics.

Typically when the stroke occurs on the left side of the brain, the right side of the body is affected. If the stroke is on the right side of the brain, the left side of the body is affected. Both have language and behavior problems. Problems with the left-brain stroke are usually aphasia and difficulty in understanding. The survivor has problems forming words, reading and writing.

Sometimes the survivor will lose the English language. However, if German was their first language, they can fluently speak that!

If the stroke is the right side of the brain, the survivor will experience similar problems. Often there is left side neglect and problems with simple tasks like dressing. Speech, reading and writing may also be affected. The patient will often have swallowing and chewing problems and have to be reminded when eating to chew their food. (It's normal to see a patient pocket their food in their mouth.) Other problems include; short attention span, outbursts of anger, inappropriate laughter or crying and loss of any musical abilities.

The best advice I could give to a family is to encourage the patient to do therapy. On occasion, I receive mail about a patient who is three years post stroke and now in a nursing home. The family is reaching out for help to see if they can get therapy for their loved one. These are survivors who are in there twenties and were so angry after their stroke that they refused to do therapy.

I can never emphasize enough that a patient has to be willing to do the therapy and follow directions from the therapist. Often it helps if the therapist talks with the family to encourage them to see what they can do facilitate the patient's motivation. Sometimes it helps to have the doctor or social worker talk to the patient. Katrina, my Occupational Therapist suggested, "If the patient can communicate in some way, have them sign a written contract that they will participate in therapy. Often this works, allowing the patient some control in the decision making. It is normal to be angry, but the patient shouldn't let their emotions interfere with their therapy," she says.

I know it's difficult because I was in the same boat, and I constantly tried to put my feelings aside in order to concentrate. Statistics show that most of the recovery is in the first six months following the stroke. I feel personally that I have reached a plateau with my recovery, yet I still see progress. Therapy in some form is an on going process.

Stroke and emotions

During ICU and rehab phase, I constantly cried which is a normal reaction of the stroke. In rehab I would frequently have bouts of crying and suddenly change to a bout of uncontrollable laughter. My therapists knew to have me sit and finish out my cycle of laughter before continuing with therapy. I experienced the inappropriate crying and laughing that has diminished slightly only because I can control it today. If I'm nervous I notice that I'll start laughing. A lot of times the family does not know how to deal with the patient's reactions and the mood swings. These suggestions may help. In my own case I wanted family and friends to just let me cry. I felt alone and there was nothing they could do to take my pain away. But if the patient can communicate after they stop crying, ask them what would comfort them.

It is said that over time emotional lability will decrease with the recovery from stroke. I have not found this to be true in my case but I am able to control it. Most people, who know me, understand what's happening when I suddenly start laughing and can't stop. Sometimes I have tears rolling down my face, and other times I have no idea what just made me laugh. I find the easiest way for me to cope is to explain to someone what's happening once I have stopped laughing or crying. Dr. Saver suggests some medications that may help with emotional lability: (1) selective Serotonin Reuptake Inhibitors, and (2) tricyclic antidepressants. He states that Baclofen has less supportive evidence and is more of a third line agent.

In the past, I always prided myself on being able to hold back a display of emotions. Now, the minute something sad comes on TV, I cry. No, I sob continuously. *Why am I crying like this?* What usually works for me is to stop and try to think of something that makes me happy. The brain is responsible for controlling our emotions, and an injury like the stroke affects our ability to control our emotions. This is just part of what happens with the stroke. Some survivors may have it, and others may not.

Post-stroke depression is a common side effect, and I hear a lot of stroke survivors trying to cope with it. During those first few months after the stroke, it's normal to feel like you are on a roller coaster with your emotions.

Both of my social workers assisted in helping me cope with these feelings and provided encouragement during my recovery. With the loss of anything, you go through the grieving process. First there is the shock of having the stroke, then you move through the different stages of denial, anger, guilt, depression and acceptance. The purpose of grieving is to allow someone to come to terms with his or her loss. This is a typical psychological process.

It's been several years since my stroke, and I still deal with bouts of depression. Depression seeps in like a tidal wave at times, magnifying situations, like yearning to wear those cute shoes from the past. It's a must that I have to talk myself through the process. *I'm disabled. I do wear a brace, and no, those shoes aren't for me.*

What I have learned about my depression is that it will pass. I acknowledge the feeling and wait until it leaves me. It's almost as if I'm having an out-of-body experience; I feel like a different person when I am no longer depressed. Although it may not be for everyone, I have found that being on a mild dose of an anti-depressant drug has helped "balance me out." There have been occasions when I have tried to wean myself off the anti-depressant only to find that I'm even more depressed. I hope I don't have to be on this medication for a lifetime, but each person is different, and only you and your doctor can decide what is best for you.

I have learned my limitations and try not to let myself get to the point of being so tired that I become angry. If I overwork myself one day, I know I'm going to pay the price the following day. Then I could become angry at something as simple as a person in the grocery store not pushing their cart through the checkout line. I become frustrated easily when I can't do something because I don't have the use of my left arm. Over the last few years I have accepted my disability, yet questions still run through my mind. *Will I have to deal with this disability the rest of my life? Is my left arm going to function normally again? How am I going to feel in ten years?* These questions do haunt me but what I *do* know is that I have today, this moment. I try to keep a positive attitude on a daily basis, but I have days when I just feel blue and nothing seems to help.

Stroke and marriage

The stroke attacks marriages too. Ninety percent of couples get divorced following a stroke. I went through another bout of depression going through my divorce. I think that anyone who faces divorce knows that it is a process. Both the stroke and divorce have made me a stronger person today. I have married couples in my stroke group where the disability has strengthened their relationship because there was a strong bond between them. Unfortunately, the opposite exists too. For example, a particular stroke survivor in my group had been a successful businessman. His wife divorced him because she felt he was no longer the man she married. They had been married for 17 years. I have heard many sad stories like this.

Stroke Support Groups

What seems to help me most with my depression is to focus on someone else and stay busy. When we focus on other people we don't have time to dwell on our own problems. That was one of my main reasons for starting a stroke support group. I encourage the people to reach out and help others. After our strokes we have feelings of worthlessness and hopelessness and by taking a baby step like doing a simple task in the group, we relieve ourselves of those feelings. I believe it has helped my recovery immensely.

The Back on Track stroke support group has been successful because of the people who have given so freely and reached out to help someone else who is going through this. I think having the support of others who have experienced what you have and can relate will help you, the stroke survivor, express your feelings whether it's depression or loneliness. In my own stroke group I have seen people come in like wounded birds and regain a life again.

While the patient is in outpatient therapy, ask the social worker if she can recommend a stroke support group. Ask if there is one that meets at the hospital. Once the patient is out of the hospital, finding support with others will help immensely. A younger stroke survivor is dealing with different issues than the older survivor, especially if there are children involved. You may have to call around for a support group that meets those needs.

Other survivors can offer so much to those who are experiencing strokes. After all, they have been down the road of dealing with this nightmare. They can offer support and encouragement along with coping skills. Sometimes the stroke survivor is not ready to be in a group, so I encourage the family to come along and listen. It helps the survivor have a close one with them the first few times before going to the group alone.

Having support from others does not eliminate the feelings of anger and frustration, but it does provide relief to know there are others who feel the same as we do, and that we are not alone. None of us expect to get 100 percent back to how we were, but each of us gives one another the encouragement to carry on. Often you realize when you listen to another survivor that someone else is struggling with even more problems. I love what Winston Churchill once said, "We make a living by what we get, but we make a life by what we give."

Out in the world

Today I'm able to enjoy many things again by taking advantage of the "handicap" provisions that come with my limitations. One is shopping.

For example, going to a mall can be exhausting. So I park as close to the store as possible in a "handicapped" parking space. Most malls have an information desk. I ask for a wheelchair. There have been times when I thought I could walk around in a mall, but found myself too tired to get back to my car. By simply asking for assistance a wheelchair can be provided and security is only too happy to help. I think that attitude plays a big part. That old familiar saying is true: *90 percent is attitude and 10 percent is just showing up for life.*

Initially my goal was to walk out of the hospital. I wanted to be whole again. Over time, and as I did outpatient rehab, my goal was to be able to adapt to living with my limitations and accept the reality. I think this is one of the hardest realities for the survivor to come to terms with, and it requires time and patience. It is a gradual process.

What exactly is a stroke?

A stroke occurs when the blood flow to the brain is interrupted by a blocked or burst blood vessel. Depending on where the damage has occurred in the brain, rehabilitation will be different for each person.

Many people are confused by the myth; "Doesn't that happen to only older people? You're too young to have had a stroke." The majority of strokes happen in people 65 and older; however it is not unusual for people at a young age to experience a stroke. There are 128,000 people under the age of 65 experiencing strokes each year. Over 700,000 Americans suffer strokes each year, making this cardiovascular disease the third leading cause of death. Stroke is the number one cause of disability. In this country someone experiences a stroke every 53 seconds. With the ongoing research and technology available today, many stroke survivors are able to lead fulfilling lives.

Suffering a stroke is an emergency and time is precious. Below the stroke warning signs are listed. If you are experiencing any of the following symptoms, call 911.

- Sudden weakness or numbness of the face or the arm and leg on one side of the body.
- Sudden dimness or a loss of vision—particularly in one or both of the eyes.
- Loss of speech or trouble talking or understanding speech.
- Sudden and severe headaches with no apparent cause.
- Unexplained dizziness, unsteadiness or sudden falls, particularly if accompanied by any of the previous symptoms.

Many people experience a TIA (transient ischemic attack). This has some of the same symptoms as stroke but lasts anywhere from five minutes to 24 hours. TIA should not be ignored, as this may be a warning signal to a larger stroke. According to the American Heart Association, a person who has a TIA is 9.5 times more likely to have a stroke.

Knowing the warning signs of stroke can reduce the damage a stroke can cause. A drug TPA (Tissue Plasminogen activator) can be administered to dissolve a clot in the brain reducing cell damage if given within the first three hours of a stroke onset. Although it is federally approved, it can only be used for *ischemic* strokes. Eighty percent of strokes are *ischemic,* where there is a blockage in the blood vessels to the brain. The other kind of stroke is *hemorrhagic,* caused by a burst or leaking blood vessel in the brain.

What is aphasia?

Some survivors have aphasia, meaning they have difficulty in speaking and understanding. Often, they can understand more than they can say. Some cannot write. "How can I help?" is a question the care-giver frequently asks. First of all, let the person with aphasia try to get the words out themselves. Try not to interrupt them. They can carry a small business size card explaining they have trouble speaking from their stroke. That way people will be patient with them. Usually people with aphasia will understand short simple sentences. (In the resource section, is listed the National Aphasia Association number which you can contact for more information.)

What can you do to prevent stroke?

What you don't know cannot only hurt you but it can kill you. Listed here are some measures you can take today to lessen your chance of a stroke. We have all heard the warning signs about smoking and putting the cigarette out. By choosing to stop you can greatly reduce your risk of cardiovascular disease. What about the birth control pill? Women need to be assertive and ask questions at the doctor's office. They should make sure the doctor discusses the risk factor. They need to find out if they are a good candidate for strokes? They need to know what steps they can take to lower their risk of cardiovascular disease. Statistics show that more women die from cardiovascular disease each year than from breast cancer.

Many women who smoke *and* take an oral contraceptive increase their risk of a stroke 22 times more than average. **Don't smoke and take birth control pills.** If you have to smoke, it is suggested that oral contraceptives be avoided. Also, there is an increased risk of birth control pills causing stroke if you have migraine headaches. Again, discuss with your doctor the risks and benefits of the birth control pill. Prior to my own stroke, I didn't ask questions. I assumed I was in good hands with my doctor. Today, I believe we must play an active role in our own health care. There are changes we can make in our lives to help prevent a stroke. We all have control over certain things. We can lose weight, stop smoking, cut back on alcohol and sodium and exercise on a regular basis. No one knows our bodies better than we do.

Turning adversity into triumph

I have gone through the same grieving process that anyone who faces an adversity has to go through. I have accepted that I'll never be the person I was. I have learned to accept that I have had a stroke. In a lot of ways, I like the new me. The lessons I have learned have been invaluable and made me a stronger, better person. I say, "thank you, God" knowing that I speak not only for myself, but for thousands of others who suffered like me. We share the common bond of moving from helplessness to triumph. In many ways the devastation in our lives is beyond our control, but the triumph through recovery and the journey to reclaim our lives is very much in our control. Although the ever present question, "why me?" may never be fully answered, one thing is for certain: God is using my life as a reminder to us all; **life is precious.** It is comforting to know that God is only a prayer away!

Kate participating in 5K walk

Letters to Kate

In this chapter, we have taken some of the letters that have been written to show how many have been touched by Kate and all that she has done. Kate receives hundreds of letters and though every one is special to her, we have randomly chosen some to be in this section. During and after Kate's ordeal, these letters have helped Kate also in her journey and all that she has been through.

Kate,

Recently, while waiting in the critical care unit of news on my father's condition, I read a magazine article, which featured your story. It was quite ironic, as my father had suffered a cerebral hemorrhage/stroke and the prognosis remains somewhat guarded. Your story has had such an impact on me and has given me hope. Let me first express to you how brave and courageous I think you are. You are quite an inspiration, and I would greatly appreciate an opportunity to speak with you personally via voice mail or eventually phone. Thank you for sharing your story I felt compelled to write to you.

My father had his stroke on September 18th and is still in a coma. They thought he would recover and suffer major physical deficits on the left side of his body. However, on day 10 he slipped into a deep coma due to swelling and lack of blood flow to other vital areas of his brain. They tell us he can definitely hear us and the surgeon believes he understands some commands. We are terrified and my greatest fear is that he is trapped inside his body and will remain in this state indefinitely. My father is 61 years old and very young and active. In addition to his will to live, the doctors have told us his survival is most likely due to the fact that his health is very good. I cling to every bit of hope and faith, but it is becoming increasingly difficult as today is exactly four weeks. I read your story daily and it brings me great comfort. In my heart, I refuse to give up hope even though I can see doctors losing hope. Please forgive me for pounding out my heart in this manner, but I feel you can understand. You didn't give up, and I feel my daddy has that same type of will to survive.

He is the most wonderful man and I would go to the ends of the earth to give him a second chance. If there is anything you can offer, advice, medical suggestions, etc., please let me know. Kate, thank you for listening and for caring about others. You will never know how reading your article at such an ironic moment helped me get through very difficult and trying times. I wish you and your family all the best and look forward to hearing from you.

Sincerely,
M. Wright

—⁓⁓—⁓⁓—⁓—

Kate,

I read your article in the stroke connection with great interest. You sure have a gift of writing. I was surprised by a few of the items like how you struggle to get going in the morning. I suppose I had/have this idea you are fired-up all the time! Your article rang true to many of my thoughts and feelings, so I congratulate you again on your ability to write in a way which allows your reader to relate.

Thanks again for being a wonderful role model and sharing so others like me can look up a little each day.

Have a great day!
M. Mohr

Hi Kate,

I have just read your article in the October Issue's of **Redbook** and wanted to let you know that I think you are an extremely brave woman, someone with whom others that may suffer from the same or similar problem could look up to and gain hope from.

Thank you,

LM

— — — —

Hi,

I just read your article about what you went through and I am truly amazed. I am a registered nurse in an emergency room and previously worked in a physical rehab unit. I was very surprised at your story and wanted to write just to say congratulations on your recovery! It is a very inspiring story and will carry it around with me to show my co-workers who still work in the rehab unit. It will be an encouragement for everyone who loses hope. I know that physical therapy and rehab is very hard work and again I congratulate you.

M.

— — — —

Dear Katie,

After e-mailing you last week about my sister-in-law, I read everything you had on line. Then I went and bought October Redbook. Thank you for sharing your story with the country. You truly are an inspiration. Keep up the good work in helping others out there. I sincerely feel a person's make-up, such as being passive or assertive (or a fighter as I call it), makes a definite difference in their recovery process. And also the type of family and support system a person has. Your family and community were wonderful.

God Bless you and yours Kate. You are remarkable.
It's nice to know it can be overcome.
 Carol, Niagara Falls, NY

—⸭— —⸭— —⸭—

Dear Kate,
 You are definitely an inspiration. My on-line friend's
husband just suffered a stroke in April. You give hope
that there is a possibility of recovery for him. I chat on
line with my friend to see how he is doing. Each little
thing he does is progress. I'm far from my friend, but I
try to keep her spirits up. Thanks for your website to help
others.
 Joy

—⸭— —⸭— —⸭—

 The first time I had heard of Kate was back in 1997
when a friend of mine had sent me the Redbook article in
which Kate's story had appeared. Since I was also a
young mother, who had suffered a stroke, I decided to
write to Kate in an effort to share similar experiences and
gain some insight into the life of someone who has gone
through some of the same things as I had. Kate had
replied, supplying me with some resources and web sites.
Some time had passed and Kate began to write again,
having gone through some of her prior correspondence.
We have been communicating by e-mail on a regular
basis ever since. In the time that had elapsed between
writing, we had again gone through similar experiences
when both Kate and I had gone through divorces, and
suffering the effects of devastating strokes. I take com-
fort, during this extremely difficult time in my life, in
knowing that someone understands what I am going

through and being able to share these thoughts and feeling with Kate.

Sincerely,

J. Bellino

—⫘—⫘—⫘—

Dear Kate,

My name is Pamela Mizzi and I live in Malta. I am studying to be a nurse. I understand how your condition was. There is a man in the ward I work in who also suffers from Locked in Syndrome and to tell you the truth I feel very sorry for the pain he is going through. He is also married with two lovely boys, and he is doing very well. He had the brain stem stroke and is paralyzed. He cries every day, thinking if he will ever recover. I am so glad that you have recovered.

He has physiotherapy and the occupational therapist visits him every day to work on exercises and he is recovering. He wanted to read your article and he loved it.

Every day he is doing wonderful progress because of you. Thank you for sharing your story, and I hope that some day this man will regain strength like you have.

Yours sincerely,

Pamela Mizzi, Malta, Europe

—⫘—⫘—⫘—

Dear Katie,

Hi my name is Karen Maschek, and I am a thirty-year-old Aussie who has just visited your website. What can I say but WOW and CONGRATULATIONS! While I know that no two strokes are the same, your story is so similar to that of a very dear friend of mine. Let me fill you in a little.

In February of this year, a friend of mine in England suffered a massive brain stem stroke. She is only 33-years-old and has an eighteen-month-old daughter and a three-year-old son. It's now seven months later and she is able to spend the weekends at home with her family.

Reading your stories posted was like looking back at the last seven months. The best part was seeing where you are at now. We keep on praying and never give up hoping that she will continue to improve, but she is finding it hard to keep that hope going. Even though I am in Australia, I communicate via email and chat programs with the husband and offer as much support, love and encouragement as I can. His strength along with their kids, is what keeps her going.

Katie, apart from wanting to send you the warmest of wishes and congratulations, I am also wondering if your booklet or video are available in other countries. I have told my friend about your website and he is excited about the chance to see a story so similar to theirs And the hope you will pass on to him and his family. I know your story will give them that extra bit of hope, as it has done for me. Warm regards to you and your family Katie and WELL DONE!

K. Maschek

Hi Katie,

I read, with great interest and admiration, the article about you in the October edition of the 1998 Red book magazine. You have been so brave throughout this entire ordeal and I know that you will someday walk again without the walker.

B. Rammes, Wisconsin

Hi Katie,

Your story is amazing! I had my stroke in July this year at the age of twenty-six. Although I am making progress, it is very slow and frustrating. Any tips on making progress? The Doctors here in England don't know much about strokes and I still don't know what caused mine. I can walk with a stick but very slowly and can't move my left arm. Any advice on recovery would be most appreciated

Best wishes,
Michelle

—⚏—⚏—⚏—

Dear Kate,

You have been such an inspiration to me. I could not begin to thank you enough. I had a hemorrhagic stroke (affecting my right side) in mid April 1999. I had several advantages over most: I have a positive outlook, I did NOT know you were NOT supposed to regain full function; and I have way too much tenacity. I was even figuring how to get better in the ambulance going to the hospital. I went on with the positive attitude for about five months. It was only then that I started into a downward spiral of depression, I even was on the verge of becoming suicidal.

I caught a TV show on Stroke Recovery. You were one of the subjects. I was thinking, "Hey, she's young, and had a much more damaging stroke than I did, has two girls to raise, and is still trying (and doing better than I at rehab!). My problems started to look a little smaller. Besides, you have all the positiveness and a good smile. It just knocked me back to my senses. I started working really hard in rehab; thinking about my daughters; and getting my life back.

I recently completed a road trip driving out to California to meet Kate and her family. I had wanted to meet her for two years after seeing her story. Kate graciously had me over for an afternoon at the beach and dinner. I've come an awful long way, all because of YOU!
Thank you Kate,
T. Cooper, Athens, GA

—∞— —∞— —∞—

Dear Kate,
I was putting my youngest child to bed tonight and I thought of you. It has been a least five years since I last saw you, and I thought, "Maybe she has a website . . ." It took all of ten seconds to find your site and I was fascinated by reading all that you have accomplished in the years since your stroke. You always were a wonderful, special and giving person and I am so excited to see how you have brought so much blessing into the lives of others who have suffered strokes.
Way to go girl! I don't know if you remember me, I was in your Bible Study group on Tuesday mornings at Hope Chapel. I now live in Thousands Oaks. I hope you are doing well, it sure looks that way from you photos. I am sure your beautiful little girls are not so little any more. Take care and God Bless you and your family.
Sincerely,
L. Warfield

—∞— —∞— —∞—

Kate,
Seven years ago, I had a stroke that effected my sensors, but not my physical mobility. I had speech

difficulties, almost a total memory loss, unable to read or write, depression, and general disorientation. My speech therapist recommended that I and my wife Gloria attend the **Back on Track Stoke Support Group.** *It was at the first meeting of this group that we first met Katie Adamson, the chairwoman of this group.*

We saw a woman, whose physical limitations were far greater than mine yet was vibrant, full of energy, and devoting her time effectively helping others. Her support and that of the group's was instrumental in getting me through some very rough emotional times. We actively participated in the group with Katie for years as I improved significantly. Even after we attended fewer meetings, we continued a close friendship.

Three years ago, tragedy struck our family again; my wife Gloria who was my active care taker, had a massive hemorrhagic stroke placing her in critical condition. It left her with a totally paralyzed right side, and unable to talk, eat or drink. She spent 105 days in a rehabilitation facility before she was released in a wheelchair and needing constant care.

During her time in the hospital and in the care center, we had many visits from Katie. She provided not only much needed emotional support but also valuable advice and information on resources.

The home care organization we used was arranged through Katie. As my wife improved we returned to the **Back on Track Stroke Support Group,** *now not only for me, but more for Gloria. These activities with Katie and the group are a mainstay of her recovery.*

I can truly say Katie's efforts and her support have been instrumental in our lives and our continued recovery from stroke.

H. Luhrs

Hello Kate,

How are you doing? Fine I hope. My name is Cheryl and I'm 39-years-old. I'm from Canada—about two hours north of Toronto. I was sitting in the dentist chair today-waiting on the dentist-when the receptionist handed me some magazines to look at. She then left the room. I started to look at some articles when your article came to me out of the blue! As I started to read the first few lines—something, I don't know what it was—told me that you had a stroke! I read on and found out that my intuitions were right! I started to weep. I found the article so inspirational that I read it a second time. I then put the magazine down and memorized your email address. I knew I had to email you the minute I got home! Ten months ago, I too had a stroke (5 TIA's and 2 major paralyzing ones on my right side). I think I'll enjoy each day for what it is! Now my goal is to help others in any way that I can. I would appreciate any suggestions that you might have regarding this. You know, it's funny how things seem to happen for a reason, isn't it? I'm glad I found you and maybe, who knows—someday, some-time, somewhere—we will meet. It is sure wonderful to know that there are others like you out there who remain so positive after all that has happened in their lives overnight, so to speak. I look forward to hearing from you Kate!

God Bless you and your family,
Cheryl

—∽—∽—∽—

Dear Kate,

Your story in Redbook was so powerful and much needed for me as my dad just had a stroke two weeks ago tonight. He is not able at this time to move his left side.

To make it a bit more intense, the day he was brought into the hospital, he was given TPA which caused massive bleeding in his neck. He has a trachea in from the surgery and is unable to speak.

I guess what I'm looking for right now is direction for us, his family. I'm just not sure what resources to tap into to get him the best care we can. After reading your story, I knew you would be able to help us.

Thank you so much for giving me hope.

H.A.

Dear Kate,

I read your article in the October edition of Redbook and I was terrified. I have suffered from severe migraines since I was thirteen. Two years ago, I was going to sleep when I lost all the feeling in the left side of my body and I was in terrible pain.

For the next several weeks, I could barely talk or walk. My GP told me that it was psychological and that I should go in to therapy. I didn't disregard this diagnosis, but I did find it a little strange. Six months ago, I saw a Neurologist that specializes in migraines and he informed me that the experience that I had was a direct result of my migraines.

Thank you for being an inspiration to everyone that reads about your experience. If there is any way that I could get involved in your cause, please let me know.

Sincerely,

K. Walsh

Ms. Kate,

I am writing to you in regards to the amazing story that I read about you in the October 1998 **Redbook** magazine. Your story has overwhelmed me, brought tears to my eyes and has also made me realize how much harder I have to fight. On January 17, 1998, my mother had a severe stroke. Like you, after three days, they told me and my father that she had a slim chance of survival. She has had a routine surgery of a heart valve replacement and two weeks later had the stroke. We were devastated. It is only my father and I am the only daughter. I am only thirty-two years old and consider both my parents my best friends. When this happened, all I could do was cry. I felt my heart had been torn into fifty million pieces. Not only to see my mother lying there, with tubes all through her and only being able to blink and move her left hand, but to also watch my father as he cried every time he left mother's room. I knew I had to be the strong one for both of them. They have always been there for and taken care of me. I had just gotten married three months prior to my mother's stroke. I went from being the happiest person on earth to the most devastated. No child could ask for more generous, giving, kind and loving parents as mine.

After several weeks, my mother did show some improvement, but no speech or no food. Her throat muscles had been severely damaged. My father and I put our lives on hold and gave complete unconditional love and time to my mother for four months. She left a rehab center here in Pittsburgh in April 1998, eating all food types, talking (few words, but actually talking) and moving her leg. It has been ten months and she can communicate fairly well. She still has no movement in her right hand or arm, but is able to walk on her own (with a cane and brace) and can talk 40% of the time with full sentences.

She is very frustrated now because she fully understands what has happened to her. We have never really gotten any answers from the medical staff of why this has happened and how do we go forward? She must get two shots a day of Lovenox for her heart value. This causes lumps, scars and bruises all in the abdomen area and thigh area where the shots must be given.

We are an average income family, but I am willing to sell my home and every asset I have to make her better again. I love my mother with all my heart and need to know that I have done all I can do to get her better. Now that she is getting a little better, I know I must now give some of my dedication to find out what else I can do.

In the beginning, it was only important to know that she knew how I loved her and needed her so. I still remember when she first went to rehab and after a few months she was so angry with me that I left her there. (I had to be the one to sign the papers and go with her in the ambulance to the rehab center, so I felt as though she had always blamed me.) But I got up in her bed and got under the blankets and told her, "Mom, you promised me you would help me raise my children, (I had planned to get pregnant right after my marriage, but held off until I knew she was okay, we plan to begin trying in the next few months) and I know you would never break a promise to me. So I need you so much right now to be strong and I need to know when my husband and I have our first child, that not only will you be by my side, you will be the first one to stand up and put our baby in your arms. Now promise me that." The very next day, my mom moved her leg and took her first step. I knew then that there truly was a God and that love can make the world go around.

I guess what I am asking, is what else can I do? Where do I turn? She has gotten to the point where she has plateaued off and I just need to know that I have looked around every corner. If you have any information, pamphlets, etc., I would be thrilled to see whatever you can send me. Ever since I read your article, I think of you and what you must have went through. I pray for your full recovery.

Thank you for your article and sharing it.

T. Murray

—ᨃ——ᨃ——ᨃ—

Dear Katie,

I am not in the habit of writing to perfect strangers, but I just finished reading the article about your incredible recovery. I wanted to take a moment to tell you that when I finished reading it, I thanked God for your husband's persistence and love for you. I admire your courage and fortitude. You must have been very, very frightened, unable to communicate, not fully understanding what had happened to you. You are a remarkable young woman, and I wish you the best that life has to offer. I have a twenty-month-old daughter myself, and even though I have full use of both of my arms, I still cannot put her hair up in a pony tail (she won't hold still long enough!).

May God Bless and Keep You and Yours Safe!

Sincerely,

S. Cooper

—ᨃ——ᨃ——ᨃ—

Dear Kate,

After reading your wonderful story, my family and I were overwhelmed with new hope for our sister. There was so much spirit and courage depicted in your mes-

sage, it has renewed our faith that there may be some hope of some recovery for her.

She had emergency surgery for a ruptured ulcer and during her stay, the doctors discovered that she was a diabetic. They kept her in the hospital an extra week to straighten out her medication and insulin needs. Two weeks later, she had a stroke. The doctor's diagnosed her with "Locked-In-Syndrome." She can only move her eyes to communicate. From her eyes down, she is paralyzed.

She has indicated to us that she feels things, but she can't move. The doctor's say she will probably not get any better, but we refuse to accept that result.

It has been six months and there has been no change in her prognosis. However, after reading your story, we know our sister has a chance. I want to thank you again for having the courage to come forth with your special story.

Sincerely,
D. Williams

Congressional speech

Before the Congress of the United States / April 23, 1997 Delivered by Kate

r. Chairman, honorable members of the Committee, it is a privilege to speak to you today. My name is Kate, I am a spokesperson for the *American Heart Association*, and most importantly, I am a mother and a wife. I know many people feel skeptical about Congress. Many people believe that government can do no good and that everything in Washington is all about the all mighty dollar. I am here to say that they are wrong. You as a body have done great things for those unfortunate people whom, through no fault of their own, are sick, and in real need of real help. The Americans with disabilities act, and the help you have given to research, to prevent, cure and lessen the effects of stroke and heart disease, are some of the finest things to ever come out of any government.

I know you face hard challenges in today's world, what you spend here; you cannot spend there. You are faced with very, very difficult choices. But, the true measures of a society, are how it treats the least of its members, how it cares for the sick and the needy.

I am only thirty-four years old, and before my devastating stroke in June, of 1995, I was a mother, a wife, an athlete and person vitally interested in my community. Now, after suffering a double brain stem pons stroke, which left me totally paralyzed, unable to even blink, and after months and months of treatment, I am still a mother, a wife, and someone vitally interested in a broader community. Only now, I am all these things but without the use of the left side of my body.

Without the funding you have already given to fight stroke and heart disease; I would be none of these things. After my stroke, I suffered from locked-in syndrome. I spent fifty days in the ICU. During those fifty days, I was conscious, I could feel everything, I could feel pain, but I could not move any part of my body. I was totally trapped in my body. Fed by a tube surgically placed in my stomach, breathing only by using a tube surgically placed in my throat, I could not speak, could not eat, could not drink, and could not move from the rigid death-like position my body had assumed.

There was little hope for me to even live through the night, and frankly, my doctor hoped I would not live, since my future seemed so bleak. I am a very lucky woman. I lived, and more than that, I overcame the locked-in syndrome.

My miracle did not come about without much prayer and great skill on the part my doctors. The knowledge and skill my doctors possessed is something that this Government, acting at its best, helped make possible. Without years of research and many dollars provided by men and women like you, I would not be here to talk to you today.

Of course, the story does not end with my leaving ICU; it only begins there. I have been through countless hours of therapy. Physical therapy has been developed to its present stage with the help of funds provided in part by this government.

I have seen my own life come to a point where I could do nothing for myself. I found myself at 33 wearing a diaper and unable to control my own bodily functions. I saw myself unable to talk for months, all the communication I had with the outside world was limited to blinking my eyes either yes or no. I will not mention the physical pain, for it was transitory.

Were you to see my daughters tears—eighteen-month-old Rachel and three-year-old Stephanie—it would be enough to convince you make research funding one of your top priorities. If you could see what this has done to my husband and other friends you would realize that stroke and heart disease is not just a problem that strikes one person, it strikes families and whole communities.

Every minute in the United States someone suffers a stroke. Annually, stroke strikes more people than cigarette smoking kills. Each year over 500,000 people have a stroke; nearly a third will die within a few months. Almost all of the survivors will be disabled for the rest of their lives.

The treatment of stroke will cost this nation over twenty-five billion dollars in medical costs and approximately two hundred billion more in lost productivity. If we hope to save Medicare, which is one of this Congress's top priorities we must learn to spend medical dollars wisely. With research we can prevent and cure stroke thus saving billions of dollars and in the bargain saving innocent people from a living death.

There is no greater good that you as a Congress could possibly do than to help the dedicated men and women who fight daily to prevent and to cure stroke and heart disease. I pray you will generously help us.

I will close by asking you to be just a little selfish, for if I can stand here today, when yesterday I was the picture of health, so can you stand here tomorrow also the victim of stroke. I pray it will not happen to you, but the truth is within the next ten years it will happen to some of you, and it may happen to all of you. So please, help, for in helping any of us, you will help all of us.

— *Kate Adamson*

Resources

Below are organizations you may want to contact for further information.

David Abrams, Esq.
ABRAMS LEGAL & MEDIATION SERVICES
Family Law
www.attorneyswithaheart.com

AMERICANS WITH DISABILITIES ACT
1-800-514-0301

AMERICAN ACADEMY OF NEUROLOGY
Search for licensed Neurologists in your area.
651-695-1940
www.aan.com

AMERICAN STROKE ASSOCIATION
7272 Greenville Ave.
Dallas, TX 75231
888-4Stroke (478-7653)
www.strokeassociation.org

AMERICAN OCCUPATIONAL THERAPY ASSOCIATION
301-948-9626
1383 Piccard Drive
Rockville, MD 20850-1725

AMERICAN PHYSICAL THERAPY ASSOCIATION
703-684-2782
111 N. Fairfax St
Alexandria, VA 22314

AMERICAN SPEECH-LANGUAGE AND HEARING ASSOCIATION
10801 Rockville Pike
Rockville, MD 20852
1-800-638-8255

ASSOCIATION FOR DRIVER REHABILITATION SPECIALISTS
Will assist individuals in finding programs in their area.
Can serve as a resource for equipment and where to get it.
1-800-290-2344
www.driver-ed.org

BRAIN INJURY ASSOCIATION
703-236-6000
www.biausa.org

KATE'S JOURNEY CONSULTING
Patients Advocacy & Assistance
1-800-641-KATE (5283)

NATIONAL APHASIA ASSOCIATION
P.O. Box 1887
Murray Hill Station
New York, Ny 10156
1-800-922-4622
www.aphasia.org

NATIONAL REHABILITATION INFORMATION CENTER
1-800-346-2742
www.naric.com

NATIONAL STROKE ASSOCIATION
9706 East Easter lane
Englewood, CO 80112
1-800-787-6537
www.stroke.org

SAFE: STROKE AWARENESS FOR EVERYONE
www.strokesafe.org
An international internet-based organization of stroke
survivors, caregivers, and medical professionals, dedicated to
providing information about and support for the challenges
presented by stroke.

JEFFREY L. SAVER, MD
Professor of Neurology
UCLA School of Medicine
710 Westwood Plaza
Los Angeles, Ca 90095

SOCAL HOME CARE
Specializing in Personal Attendants
1-800-707-8781
www.socalhomecare.com

STROKE ASSOCIATION OF SOUTHERN CALIFORNIA
2001 S Barrington Avenue #308
Los Angeles, CA 90025
310-575-1699
www.strokesocal.org

STROKE CAREGIVERS HANDBOOK
www.strokesafe.org/ndbook.html

STROKE CONNECTION MAGAZINE
1-800-553-6321
Speak to survivors and caregivers of stroke. Find a local stroke group in your area.
Email: strokeconnection@heart.org

THE STROKE NETWORK, INC.
Listening, understanding, supporting stroke survivors and caregivers
www.strokenetwork.org

WELL SPOUSE FOUNDATION
1-800-838-0879
www.wellspouse.org

About the Author

*N*ew Zealand born Kate Adamson lives in Los Angeles, California with her family. Since her devastating stroke in 1995, Kate has accomplished more than anyone ever imagined. She has testified on behalf of the American Heart Association, before the United States Congress for more funding for stroke and heart research. Kate is a national spokesperson for the American Stroke Association and has served as a board member of the South Bay American Heart Association in Los Angeles. She was appointed to the University of Southern California, Department of Biokinesiology and Physical Therapy Board of Counselors.

Kate is a sought after inspirational keynote speaker and has inspired countless people around the country with her story. The lessons she learned are a model for anyone who feels their goals and dreams are sometimes out of reach. Kate teaches others to overcome any situation and how to move forward with any challenge by continually focusing on what you can do. Her story has been featured in various magazines, including *Vim & Vigor, Caregiver, Keeping Well, Stroke Smart and Stroke Connection, The Female Patient* and *Redbook.*

Kate is a constant source for the media, appearing on numerous radio and TV interviews including both local and national outlets. She has appeared on the Fox News Channel, The O'Reilly Factor, CBS Sunday morning news, The Abrams Report, MSNBC, ABC, NBC, 700 Club, Coral Ridge Ministries and the Trinity Broadcast Network (TBN) with Jay Jones on the Joy program. She is a tireless advocate for patient's rights and is a devoted advocate for women's health care issues.

—⁓——⁓——⁓—

Kate is available for speaking engagements at conferences, conventions and business meetings. She can be reached by visiting her website at **www.katesjourney.com.**